Sadlier

CHRIST IN US™

Parish Edition 6

"*Christ In Us* Grade 6 cover artwork speaks to the students' discovery of the importance of their witness to the love found in the salvation of Jesus Christ."

Reverend Donald Senior, C.P., S.T.D.

Sadlier Religion

This advanced publication copy has been printed prior to final publication and pending ecclesiastical approval.

Acknowledgments

This publication was printed with permission pending from the following copyright holders.

Excerpts from the *Catechism of the Catholic Church, second edition,* © 2000, Libreria Editrice Vaticana—United States Conference of Catholic Bishops, Washington, D.C. All rights reserved.

Scripture texts in this work are taken from the *New American Bible, revised edition* © 2010, 1991, 1986, 1970 Confraternity of Christian Doctrine, Washington, D.C. All Rights Reserved. No part of the *New American Bible* may be reproduced in any form without permission in writing from the copyright owner.

Excerpts from the English translation of *The Roman Missal* © 2010 International Commission on English in the Liturgy, Inc. (ICEL). All rights reserved.

Excerpts from the English translation of *The Liturgy of the Hours* © 1974, ICEL. All rights reserved.

Excerpts from the English translation of *Rite of Penance* © 1974, ICEL. All rights reserved.

Excerpts from the English translation of Rite of Christian Initiation of Adults © 1985, ICEL. All rights reserved.

Excerpts from *Catholic Household Blessings and Prayers (Revised Edition)* © 1988, 2007, United States Catholic Conference, Inc. Washington, D.C. All rights reserved.

Quotations from papal addresses, audiences, homilies, speeches, messages, meditations, encyclicals, and other Vatican documents are from www.vatican.va and copyright © by Libreria Editrice Vaticana or Secretaria pro Communicatione.

His Holiness Pope Francis, Twitter posts: November 1, 2017, 5:30 a.m., November 12, 2017, 4:30 a.m., and November 14, 2017, 4:30 a.m. http://twitter.com/Pontifex

Excerpts from the Web sites of the Homiletic and Pastoral Review, sensAgent, the Society of Saint Gianna Beretta Molla, the United States Conference of Catholic Bishops, My Jewish Learning, and the Jesuit Institute © 2018. All rights reserved.

Excerpt from *Life of Saint Columba* © 1991 by Penguin Books Ltd.

Excerpt from Bert Ghezzi, *The Voices of the Saints* © 2000 by Doubleday.

Excerpts from Fulton J. Sheen, *Remade for Happiness: Achieving Life's Purpose Through Spiritual Transformation,* Ignatius Press, San Francisco. Copyright © 1946 by P.J. Kenedy & Sons.

Excerpts from *Sermon in a Sentence: A Treasury of Quotations on the Spiritual Life. Vol. 2: St. Francis de Sale*s. Selected and arranged by John P. McClernon. © 2003 Ignatius Press, San Francisco.

Excerpts from Saints on Series: Vol II by Rory Michael Fox © 2012 by E-Saint Library.

Excerpts from *The Joy in Loving: A Guide to Daily Living by Mother Teresa* compiled by Jaya Chaliha and Edward Le Joly, Penguin Group © Jaya Chaliha and Edward Le Joly, 1996.

William H. Sadlier, Inc.
9 Pine Street
New York, NY 10005-4700

ISBN: 978-0-8215-3696-4

2 3 4 5 6 7 8 9 WEBC 23 22 21

Christ In Us was developed in collaboration with the wisdom of the community. The team included respected catechetical, liturgical, pastoral, and theological experts who shared their insights and inspired its development.

With grateful acknowledgment of
William Sadlier Dinger and Frank Sadlier Dinger
for their leadership, vision, and commitment to excellence in the development
of Sadlier's catechetical programs and resources since 1963

Theological and Liturgical Consultants

Most Reverend Christopher James Coyne
Bishop of Burlington, VT

Donna Eschenauer, Ph.D.
Associate Dean, Associate Professor of
    Pastoral Theology
St. Joseph's Seminary and College

Rita Ferrone, M.Div.

Thomas Kendzia
Sadlier National Consultant for
    Liturgy and Music

Reverend Monsignor John Pollard, M. Ed. S.T.L.
Alissa Thorell, M.T.S

John B. Angotti, M.A.P.S.

Barbara Sutton, D.Min.

Kathleen Dorsey Bellow, D.Min.

Scripture Consultant

Reverend Donald Senior, C.P., S.T.D.
Chancellor and President Emeritus
    Catholic Theological Union

Catechetical Consultants

Amy Welborn, M.A.

Susan Stark

Sr. Theresa Engel, O.S.F.
Member of the School Sisters of St. Francis

Maureen A. Kelly, M.A.

Karla Manternach, M.A.

Woodeene Koenig-Bricker, M.A.

Connie Clark

Shannon Chisholm, Ph.D.

Susan M. Sink

Maureen Shaughnessy, S.C.

Lori Dahlhoff, Ed.D.

Andrea D. Chavez-Kopp, M.Ed.

Educational Consultants

Richard Culatta

Heidi Hayes Jacobs, Ed.D.

Jay McTighe

Allie Johnston

Learning Style Inclusion Consultants

Charleen Katra, M.A.

Jennifer Ochoa, M.Ed., LDT/C

Inculturation Consultants

Luis J. Medina
Director, Bilingual Catechesis

Charlene Howard, M.A.

Michael P. Howard, M.A.
Eat the Scroll Ministry

Catholic Social Teaching

Kristin Witte, D.Min.

Genevieve Jordan Laskey, M.A.

Michael Jordan Laskey, M.A.

Media and Technology Consultants

Spirit Juice Studios

Top Floor Productions

Sr. Caroline Cerveny, S.S.J.-T.O.S.F., D.Min.

Contents

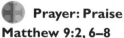

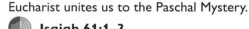

Your Spiritual Journey

Your Grade 6 Saint:
Saint Dominic

Christ In Us offers a saint for every grade. As you journey through each unit, remember to pray to your grade's saint. Ask him or her to help guide you to be closer to Jesus Christ.

Saint Dominic de Guzmán was born in Castile, Spain in 1170 into a wealthy and devout Catholic family with strong ties to the Church. His father was lord of the manor in his village, which meant that he owned most of the land. His uncle was an archbishop.

In 1191, Spain was devastated by famine. At that time, Dominic was studying to become a priest and was not as affected as other families by the hunger and suffering. He did understand the suffering felt by other people and decided to give away his money and sold his clothes, furniture and books to help feed the hungry. Dominic's fellow students asked him why he would do something that left him without almost all he owned. Dominic said, "Would you have me study off these dead skins, when men are dying of hunger?" The "dead skins" Dominic mentioned referred to the clothing people wore, since animal skins were often used to make the clothing, such as coats and hats.

Soon after Dominic was ordained a priest, he saw a need to help preach God's Word in Europe's growing cities. Dominic believed that a new kind of spiritual organization in the Church would help minister to its members through an example of poverty and a system of education. Together with six followers, Dominic began his mission in Toulouse, France.

Dominic believed his group's mission to preach the Gospel depended on a new kind of spirituality for his followers. It was one based on a life of contemplative prayer and penance.

In 1216, Church leaders recognized Dominic's religious organization as The Order of Preachers. They are more commonly known today as the Dominicans.

How can you show others that you are a follower of Jesus Christ?

Welcome to **Christ In Us**, an exciting way to grow in your Catholic faith!

Each one of us is on a journey to love and know Jesus Christ. Imagine if every person who met you knew you were a friend of Christ!

Together in this program

we will **ENCOUNTER** Jesus Christ

we will **ACCOMPANY** him in our lives

we will **WITNESS** to our faith.

You will use this book as well as your online digital portal as you discover and grow closer to Jesus Christ.

As you journey in your faith, you can think about these questions:

"I myself am the bread of life. No one who comes to me shall ever be hungry, and no one who believes in me shall ever thirst."

John 6:35

How does your faith, the Church, and your family help bring you closer to God?

Why is it important to have Christ live in you?

What would happen if you did not have Jesus in your life?

Every lesson has four Spiraling Main Ideas.
Here is an example.

Each lesson has one or more **Faith Words** to help you understand the important words we use as Catholics.

Be sure to look at all the wonderful photos and beautiful art found in the pages of your book.

Mary cooperated fully in God's plan of salvation.

Long ago, there lived a young woman named Mary in a town called Nazareth. Mary, who was a virgin, was engaged to a man named Joseph. One day, the angel Gabriel appeared to Mary. He greeted her with the words "Hail, favored one! The Lord is with you" (Luke 1:28).

At this event, called the Annunciation, Gabriel continued by saying: "Do not be afraid, Mary, for you have found favor with God. Behold, you will conceive in your womb and bear a son, and you shall name him Jesus. He will be great and will be called Son of the Most High, . . . and of his kingdom there will be no end" (Luke 1:30–33).

Mary asked the angel: "How can this be?" The angel replied: "The holy Spirit will come upon you, and the power of the Most High will overshadow you. Therefore the child to be born will be called holy, the Son of God" (Luke 1:35). Out of all women everywhere and at all times, God had chosen Mary to be the mother of his divine Son. God had been preparing Mary for this role in salvation history ever since the very moment of her conception in the body of her mother. Mary is unique among all people in that she was conceived without the stain of Original Sin. We call this the **Immaculate Conception**. Mary also remained pure from all personal sin throughout her life.

Faith Word

Immaculate Conception see p. 257

How does my faith help me make decisions and choices?

Did You Know?

 Mary is with us today.

As you explore this question, you might be asked to stop and think more about it and then do a short **Activity** to answer it better.

 **A**ctivity

The first part of the Hail Mary prayer recalls the Annunciation. Explain in your own words what each line means.

Hail Mary _____

Full of grace _____

The Lord is with you _____

Blessed are you among women _____

And blessed is the fruit of your womb, Jesus _____

Now, tell the account of the Annunciation to a friend, using the words you wrote above. Then, pray the Hail Mary together.

44   ACCOMPANY

You will be asked to **Show What You Know** by writing the answers to some short questions pertaining to the lesson.

You will not be alone as you journey through **Christ In Us**. You will have lots of **Partners in Faith**—saints and other holy people who lived amazing lives—walking with you.

Along with Saint Dominic, here are some other Partners in Faith whom you will meet throughout the book!

Ruth and Naomi

Saint Stephen

Saint Joan of Arc

Saint Charles Lwanga

Saint John XXIII

Archbishop Fulton Sheen

Saint Frances Xavier Cabrini

Saint Francis de Sales

Next, you will be asked to go to your **Portfolio** to creatively share how you can bring Christ to the world.

Each lesson ends with a **Mini-Task** that invites you to show ways you can live out your faith as a missionary disciple of Christ.

Finally, you will be given ways to think and talk with your family **At Home**.

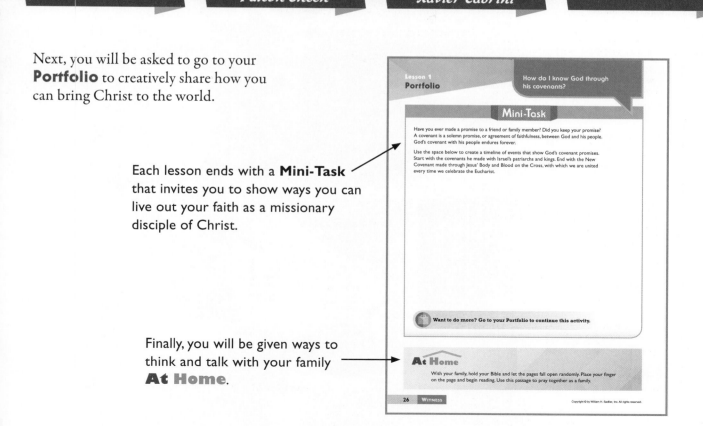

Lesson 1
Portfolio

How do I know God through his covenants?

Mini-Task

Have you ever made a promise to a friend or family member? Did you keep your promise? A covenant is a solemn promise, or agreement of faithfulness, between God and his people. God's covenant with his people endures forever.

Use the space below to create a timeline of events that show God's covenant promises. Start with the covenants he made with Israel's patriarchs and kings. End with the New Covenant made through Jesus' Body and Blood on the Cross, with which we are united every time we celebrate the Eucharist.

Want to do more? Go to your Portfolio to continue this activity.

At Home

With your family, hold your Bible and let the pages fall open randomly. Place your finger on the page and begin reading. Use this passage to pray together as a family.

Christ In Us features an online portal filled with exciting media and activities to go with the lessons in your book. If you see one of these icons below in your book, you know it's time to visit the student portal for more. (Note: Not every icon will appear in your book.)

 Participate in lesson prayers, whose words are online and downloadable

Learn more about the lesson's **Did You Know?** topic by watching an interesting video and doing an activity

 Learn more about the lesson's **Partner in Faith** by watching an online video and completing the activity that follows

Listen to Scripture verses and Catholic prayers and learn them by heart

 Find fun activities to share and recall what you have learned

Show What You Know by completing online assessments

 Read and remember the **Faith Words** definitions

Complete projects and tasks in the online **Portfolio** or *Portfolio Workbook*

 Listen to the songs for your grade level and sing along!

Your Songs for Grade 6	
Unit Songs	**Liturgical Catechesis Seasonal Songs**
Unit 1: "We Have Been Told," David Haas	**Advent:** "Christ, Circle Round Us," Daniel Schutte/OCP
Unit 2: "Light of Christ," Tom Kendzia/OCP	**Christmas:** "Hark! The Herald Angels Sing," PD
Unit 3: "I Send You Out," John Angotti	**Easter:** "This Is The Day," Tom Kendzia/OCP
Unit 4: "Here I Am, Lord," Daniel Schutte/OCP	**Pentecost:** "Holy Spirit Come Now," Manibusan/OCP
Unit 5: "We Are Called," David Haas	

Your journey continues with your login to *Christ In Us* Digital!

Here you can explore all the exciting resources that blend together with your textbook.

Take a look at your personalized online dashboard. Everything you need is at your fingertips!

- Think of your portfolio as your digital backpack! Here you can get your assignments, see reminders, send emails, and even talk to your catechist.

- Interactive Mini-Tasks enable you to share exciting activities with others. You will be able to get hands on and creative by making videos or interactive posters.

- Listen with your heart and pray the prayers of *Lectio* and *Visio Divina*, praise, petition, intercession, traditional, thanksgiving, and meditation from your lesson.

- Track your progress with digital quizzes and tests.

Have a wonderful year!

Unit 1
The Faith Professed

The Last Supper

Unit Prayer

Leader: Saint Dominic believed that through a life of prayer, study, preaching, and community, we would be able to live his prayer: "We must sow the seed, not keep it for ourselves." He lived so that others might know and understand God's presence. By doing small things in Christ's name, we can change the world. We, too, become evangelists!

Let us listen to how Jesus' love and presence is made known through modern evangelists among us. Listen to the stories of missionary disciples among us.

Leader: Let us pray:
Lord Jesus, help us to know you in our daily lives. We want to be living witnesses of your love for us and to be evangelists! Teach us to live just as Saint Dominic taught us to share your love in our world.

Leader: For the time and place for daily prayer:

All: O God, help us to sow your seeds in the world.

Leader: For the gift of your Word in Sacred Scripture that feeds us with wisdom:

All: O God, help us to sow your seeds in the world.

Leader: For the strength to act and speak as you have taught us:

All: O God, help us to sow your seeds in the world.

Leader: For the gift of those who love us:

All: O God, help us to sow your seeds in the world.

(*End the Unit Prayer by singing the song for this unit.*)

Unit Song: "We Have Been Told," David Haas

Missionary Discipleship

Can you think of a time when you had to do the right thing? Have you ever had to "stand up" for someone who was being bullied or made fun of? How did you feel?

How do we know God?

Throughout all of salvation history, God has never stopped inviting us to know him and to share in his life and love. God has revealed himself to us through his covenants, through Sacred Scripture, and through his Son, Jesus Christ. We also come to know God through the Church, to whom Jesus entrusted the power and authority to teach the faith.

 Go to the digital portal for a *Lectio* **and** *Visio Divina* **prayer.**

"You are indeed Holy, O Lord,
and from the world's beginning
are ceaselessly at work,
so that the human race may become holy,
just as you yourself are holy."

Eucharistic Prayer for Reconciliation

Throughout all history God has made himself known to us.

Gradually, God, in his goodness and wisdom, revealed himself to us. Throughout history, God has made known his loving plan of salvation. Salvation history is the account of God's enduring love for us as he reveals who he is in stages and invites us to respond.

God's Revelation began when he created the world and everything in it. We can know who God is through the things that he has created. God is the origin and the end of everything.

God created our first parents, Adam and Eve, in his own image and likeness. From the very beginning, God revealed himself to them. He invited them into relationship with him. Even when they sinned and turned away from him, God never stopped loving them. God's love was so great that he promised them **salvation**. Salvation is the forgiveness of sin and the restoration of relationship with God. He also offered them his **covenant**, a solemn agreement of faithfulness between God and his people.

We find the stories of God's covenants in the Old Testament. The covenants God made with Noah, Abraham, and Moses reveal his faithfulness and love, and show us that he will always be with us. They prepared God's people for Jesus, the new and everlasting covenant.

Faith Words

salvation see p. 259

covenant see p. 257

What is one way I have been faithful to a promise in my life?

Did You Know?

The Bible is available online and in apps.

God's Covenant with Noah: Genesis 9:9–17
God promised that even if humanity failed him again, he would never send another flood to destroy life on earth. The symbol of this promise was a rainbow. This Scripture account revealed an important religious truth: God's mercy, not death and destruction, will have the final word.

God's Covenant with Abraham: Genesis 17:1–2
God chose Abraham to be the father of his people. By the covenant he established with Abraham, God would give him a son and make a great nation of him.

God's Covenant with Moses: Exodus 19:4–6
God chose Moses to lead his people out of slavery and to guide his people to freedom. Through Moses, God established a personal relationship with the Israelites and revealed his law to them.

The covenants of the Old Testament lead to Jesus. He is the new and everlasting covenant who will lead us to salvation.

> "See, days are coming—oracle of the LORD—when I will make a new covenant with the house of Israel and the house of Judah. . . . I will place my law within them, and write it upon their hearts; I will be their God, and they shall be my people.'"
>
> Jeremiah 31:31–33

Activity

The Bible tells us about our ancestors in faith. Complete the following chart using the information in your book and what you already know. Discuss with a partner.

Ancestor in faith	Covenant/ Promise	Truth about God	Result for humanity	How Jesus completes this for us
Noah				
Abraham				
Moses				

Sacred Scripture is the Word of God.

The word *Scripture* means "holy writings." Sacred Scripture is the Word of God expressed in human words. Inspired by the Holy Spirit, human writers put down on paper what God wanted us to know about himself. They shared the account of God's plan to bring us back to him through Christ Jesus. God is the true author of Sacred Scripture because he inspired its human authors.

The forty-six books of the Old Testament and the twenty-seven books of the New Testament reveal the truth about God's love for us.

The Books of the Bible

The Old Testament

- The Pentateuch is the first five books of the Bible. These books tell the story of Creation, of God revealing himself to his Chosen People and establishing a covenant with them.
- The historical books are sixteen books that tell of how God's people lived the covenant. Sometimes God's people did well, and sometimes they fell short.
- The wisdom books contain wise teachings about the covenant with God. There are seven wisdom books.
- The prophetic books contain the words of the prophets. These eighteen books call God's people to be faithful to the covenant. They also remind the people that God has always been faithful to them.

The New Testament

- The Gospels have at their center Jesus Christ. In the four Gospels we encounter the mystery of Christ's life, Death, Resurrection, and Ascension.
- The Acts of the Apostles recounts the life of the early Church.
- The New Testament letters, also known as the thirteen Epistles, were written by Saint Paul. In them we read about the Christian faith and how to live as followers of Jesus.
- The Catholic Epistles are eight additional letters that teach about our faith.
- The Book of Revelation is the final book in the Bible. It anticipates the end times and encourages Christians to remain faithful to God, even when it is difficult or dangerous to do so.

Activity

Your class will be organized into two groups: one to discuss the Old Testament and one to discuss the New Testament. Work with your group to create clues about your section of the Bible. Write the clues on index cards, and use them to play a trivia game with the whole class.

What Makes Us Catholic?

Not all Bibles are alike. Catholic Bibles have seven more books than other Christian Bibles. These books are called *deuterocanonical*. They are all in the Old Testament and contain accounts of God's interactions with the people of Israel. At first, all Christians used the same books. Then some Christians left these books out of the canon, or the official list of the books of the Bible, because they were not written in Hebrew. Catholics kept them in, believing them to be inspired by the Holy Spirit. These seven books are Tobit, Judith, Wisdom, Sirach, Baruch, 1 Maccabees, and 2 Maccabees.

Jesus is the fullness of Divine Revelation.

After the Fall, when Adam and Eve turned away from God, he did not give up on humanity. Instead, God began to gather his people to himself. The covenants God made with Noah, Abraham, and Moses were God's response to the chaos caused by sin. God told his people: "I will take you as my own people, and I will be your God; and you will know that I, the LORD, am your God" (Exodus 6:7).

The People of Israel often struggled to keep God's covenant. Through his prophets, God assured them that even though they often failed him, he had a plan for their salvation. A **New Covenant** would replace the old. This New Covenant would last forever.

In the Gospels, we encounter Jesus Christ, who tells his disciples at the Last Supper: "This cup is the new covenant in my blood, which will be shed for you" (Luke 22:20). Jesus is the fullness of Divine Revelation. Through Jesus, God the Father fulfilled his plan of salvation and established his everlasting covenant.

Faith Word

New Covenant see p. 258

One Church, Many Cultures

Catholics of all ages have a responsibility to share and celebrate their faith. Young people can do their part by sharing their faith with one another and with the wider world. Every year, the Church celebrates World Youth Day in a different city, usually over the summer. Catholic young people from different cultures and backgrounds all over the world join together to pray and to learn more about their faith from priests, catechists, youth leaders, and even the pope. They learn from one another, too.

"Listen, that you may have life. I will make with you an everlasting covenant, the steadfast loyalty promised to David."

Isaiah 55:3

Sacred Tradition began with the preaching of the Apostles.

Imagine yourself as one of Jesus' first followers. Throughout Jesus' ministry, you have walked the roads with him. You have listened, watched, prayed, and had engaging conversations.

Jesus' teaching and presence have touched you deeply. Jesus has totally changed your life. You know, in a very deep way, that you have met the Lord. Your life is different now, because you know Jesus. How would others, in the centuries to come, be able to have the same experience?

As we know, Jesus fulfilled the Father's plan of salvation for us through his life, Death, Resurrection, and Ascension. God continues to offer his salvation to the world through his Church, the Body of Christ. In order for this to happen, Christ commanded his Apostles to preach the Gospel. Inspired by the Holy Spirit, they communicated the message of salvation through their preaching and in writing.

The Apostles would, in turn, hand on to their successors the preaching and teaching that Christ had entrusted to them. This process of passing on the Gospel message, from Christ to the Apostles to their successors, is called Sacred Tradition. The Apostles entrusted the Church with the responsibility to

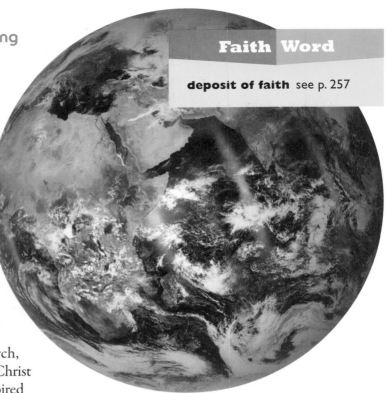

Faith Word

deposit of faith see p. 257

profess and guard the **deposit of faith** contained in Sacred Scripture and Sacred Tradition. From the time of the Apostles, the Church has passed on the Good News of salvation in her life, teaching, and worship. The Church will continue to carry out this sacred mission until Christ returns in glory.

Partners in Faith

Saint Dominic

Saint Dominic was born in Spain. He lived about the same time as Saint Francis of Assisi. When he was about 25 years old, he became a priest. Several years later, he and six other priests began traveling around and preaching the Gospel. They became known as the Order of Preachers. Today, we call them Dominicans, after Saint Dominic. Dominic said that it was important to study and pray as well as to preach.

 Learn more about the life of Saint Dominic.

Faith Words

salvation	covenant
New Covenant	deposit of faith

 Show What You Know

Explain each term in your own words.

1. deposit of faith

sacred scripture and sacred tradition passed on in the church

2. covenant

Noah was one, which is basically a deal,

3. salvation

Jesus forgives us our sins

4. New Covenant

Now jesus gives us comunion through jesus, That our deal with go

Live Your Faith

What Scripture verse or passage inspires you to live God's covenant faithfully?

What is a promise you can make to God right now?

Mini-Task

Have you ever made a promise to a friend or family member? Did you keep your promise? A covenant is a solemn promise, or agreement of faithfulness, between God and his people. God's covenant with his people endures forever.

Use the space below to create a timeline of events that shows God's covenant promises. Start with the covenants he made with Israel's patriarchs and kings. End with the New Covenant made through Jesus' Body and Blood on the Cross, with which we are united every time we celebrate the Eucharist.

 Want to do more? Go to your Portfolio to continue this activity.

At Home

With your family, hold your Bible and let the pages fall open randomly. Place your finger on the page and begin reading. Use this passage to pray together as a family.

Who is God?

From the time of the first people, humanity has wondered: Who is God? We want to know the answer to this question because we were created with a desire to know and love God and to serve him. God created us to share in his life and to follow his plan for our lives. Only this will make us truly happy. God the Father, God the Son, and God the Holy Spirit together continue the work of creation. God also guides the Church in carrying out her divine mission.

 Go to the digital portal for a prayer of praise.

"The spirit of the LORD GOD is upon me,
   because the LORD has anointed me;
He has sent me to bring good news to
   the afflicted,
      to bind up the brokenhearted,
To proclaim liberty to the captives,
   release to the prisoners."

Isaiah 61:1

Jesus Christ is the fullness of Divine Revelation.

In the Book of Genesis, God speaks to us about creation in human language. We learn many important truths. First, we learn that God created the entire universe out of nothing.

Faith Word

Divine Revelation see p. 257

"God created mankind in his image; in the image of God he created them; male and female he created them."

Genesis 1:27

We also learn that everything God created is good and depends on him, and that all creation, especially humankind, reveals the glory of God.

We are the high point of God's creation. He created us with a body and a soul and gave us the gift of free will—the freedom and ability to choose between good and evil—and with a conscience. He created us with the ability to reason, to think, to love, and to form relationships. Of all God's creatures, only human beings are able to know and love their Creator. In fact, it is for that very purpose that God created us.

God has never stopped communicating his goodness, truth, and love, and his desire for us to respond to that love. God's **Divine Revelation** began with the creation of Adam and Eve and their descendants. Even when our first parents turned away from God, he did not abandon humanity. Instead, he revealed a loving plan to save us and to allow us to share in his divine life.

Why is it good that I have a purpose in my life?

Did You Know?

The Grace Before Meals began with the early Christians.

French artist Marc Chagall captures the Scripture event (Exodus 3:1–22) of how God reveals himself to Moses. In the painting, Moses falls to his knees before a burning bush. An angel emerges from within a colorful circle and tells Moses of his mission to lead the Israelites to freedom.

God's Revelation continued through the history of the ancient Israelites, beginning with the patriarchs. The drama of God's abiding presence with his people and his plan to bring them back to him unfolds throughout the Old Testament. God is faithful. He never abandons his people.

In the Book of Exodus, God tells Moses: "I am the God of your father, . . . the God of Abraham, the God of Isaac, and the God of Jacob" (Exodus 3:6). God explains that he has seen his people's suffering and has come to rescue them.

Moses then asks God the question that humanity has been asking since the beginning of time: *Who are you?* God tells Moses: "I am who I am." He instructs Moses to tell the Israelites "I AM has sent me to you" (Exodus 3:14). In saying his name, God gives us a glimpse into the mystery of who he is. God is the one who is, who was, and who will be.

After Moses, God continued to speak to our ancestors in faith. Through the prophets, God prepared his people for the clearest revelation of himself in his Son, Jesus Christ.

"So whoever is in Christ is a new creation: the old things have passed away; behold, new things have come."

2 Corinthians 5:17

What Makes Us Catholic?

We are all called to live holy lives of love and service to God and others. The Church honors as saints those who have lived this call in a heroic way. The process by which a person is officially declared a saint is called *canonization.* Throughout the Church's history, thousands of men and women have been named as saints. They include Jesus' first followers; martyrs, or those who died for their faith; priests, bishops, and popes; religious brothers and sisters; and people from all walks of life.

The Blessed Trinity continues the work of creation.

God's work of creation continues today through all Three Persons of the Blessed Trinity—God the Father, God the Son, and God the Holy Spirit. The mystery of the Blessed Trinity is the central mystery of our faith. It is not something that we could ever figure out on our own. Rather, only God could make this mystery known to us by revealing himself as Father, Son, and Holy Spirit.

The saving work of the Trinity is both communal and personal. We know that the Persons of the Trinity are one. Yet, in carrying out the work of salvation, each Person of the Trinity operates in distinct ways. We come to know God the Father and are saved "through" God the Son, who is Jesus Christ, and "in" God the Holy Spirit. This is why, during the Mass, we often address the Father "through" Jesus Christ the Son and "in" the Holy Spirit. It is important to remember that when we speak about God, we mean all Three Persons of the Blessed Trinity. This is because the Father, the Son, and the Holy Spirit are One God in Three Persons.

God has no beginning or end. The Son of God was present with God the Father and God the Holy Spirit from all eternity. Likewise, God the Holy Spirit was present with God the Father and God the Son from all eternity. The image of "a mighty wind" moving over the water in the account of Creation refers to the Spirit or Breath of God (see Genesis 1:1–2).

Jesus Christ and the Holy Spirit are one with the Father. In other words, the Three Divine Persons are inseparable both in who they are (God) and in what they do. Their common mission is to bring all of humanity into communion with the Blessed Trinity. The Incarnation of Jesus, the Son of God, and the sending of the Holy Spirit accomplish this saving work.

One Church, Many Cultures

The Church is universal and includes people from different cultures who all celebrate the same faith. The Church honors the cultural traditions and diversity of her members. In the United States, Native American Catholics include native symbols, blessings, songs, and dances in their celebrations, and they participate in special meals and sunrise Masses. In 2012, Saint Kateri Tekakwitha, an Algonquin-Mohawk woman, became the first Native American to be canonized. The annual Kateri Conference invites Native American Catholics from around the country to celebrate their faith together.

Jesus is the long-awaited Messiah.

For many centuries, God had been preparing his people to look forward to the coming of a messiah. This messiah would bring salvation to the **People of God**. Those who were familiar with the writings of the prophets would know that God was sending a messenger to prepare the way for the Messiah (see Mark 1:2).

In the New Testament, we read about that messenger: John the Baptist. John invited people to repent—to change their lives. He was preparing them for the Messiah. *Messiah* is the Hebrew word for "Christ," a Greek word. Both *Christ* and *messiah* mean "anointed one." In ancient Israel, kings, priests, and prophets were anointed with oil to indicate that God had chosen them for a special purpose. Jesus Christ, the **Messiah** God sent to his people, would be anointed by the Spirit of the Lord as priest, prophet, and king. He would save God's people.

In Luke's Gospel, the angel who announced the birth of Jesus to the shepherds identified Jesus as the messiah promised to Israel: "For today in the city of David a savior has been born for you who is Messiah and Lord" (Luke 2:11).

Years later, Jesus began his public life and ministry after his baptism by John in the Jordan River. His baptism would also reveal that he was the Messiah.

> "On coming up out of the water he saw the heavens being torn open and the Spirit, like a dove, descending upon him. And a voice came from the heavens, 'You are my beloved Son; with you I am well pleased.'"
>
> Mark 1:10–11

Finally, Jesus' followers would come to know that he was the Messiah, "the Holy One of God" (Mark 1:24), through his words and deeds.

Faith Words

People of God see p. 258

Messiah see p. 258

Activity

Write three names for Jesus and what they mean.

1. _____

2. _____

3. _____

Write a song or poem that explains who Jesus is, using the three names. Share your song or poem with a partner or the group.

The Church is called to bring the Good News of salvation to all people.

The mission of the Church is to evangelize the world so that all may know the saving love of God. As members of the Church, we too are called to be witness to God's love and mercy.

The word *church* means "a gathering of people or community for worship." From the beginning, God has been gathering his people to himself in order to share his divine life with us.

Then came Jesus Christ, God the Father's only divine Son. Jesus' whole life—his preaching, teaching, and witness—was the Good News of salvation. Christ freed us from sin and made it possible for us to participate in the very life of God. Jesus also promised that his Father and he would send the Holy Spirit to teach and guide us in the truth.

After his Resurrection, Jesus appeared to his disciples and said: "'Peace be with you. As the Father has sent me, so I send you.' And when he had said this, he breathed on them and said to them, 'Receive the holy Spirit'" (John 20:20–22).

On the day of Pentecost, the Holy Spirit descended upon the Apostles and the Church. Ever since then, the Holy Spirit has been building up the Church throughout the world.

The saving work of the Blessed Trinity brought the Church into being. Today, the Church continues to preach the Gospel, as Jesus did, and to share in the very life of the Trinity.

Activity

The Church has a mission. Write a mission statement for the Church. Turn to a partner and explain your mission statement.

_____

_____

_____

_____

_____

Partners in Faith

Ruth and Naomi

Ruth and Naomi lived in Israel many centuries before Jesus. Ruth and Naomi are our ancestors in faith. Ruth was married to Naomi's son. After he died, Naomi told Ruth to return to her own family. Ruth refused because Naomi had taught her about the God of Israel. Ruth told Naomi: "Your God [will be] my God" (Ruth 1:16). Together they traveled to Bethlehem. There, Ruth worked in the fields picking barley. Eventually she married a man named Boaz, but she always cared deeply for Naomi. Ruth is the great-grandmother of King David, from whose family Jesus, the Messiah, would be born many centuries later.

 Learn more about the lives of Ruth and Naomi.

Faith Words

Messiah   **People of God**   **Divine Revelation**

 Show What You Know

Draw a line to match each term to its definition.

1. Messiah

2. Divine Revelation

3. humans

4. People of God

5. Blessed Trinity

the people God has been gathering to himself to share in his life

Jesus, who was anointed to bring salvation to the People of God

the way God reveals himself to us

the high point of God's creation

God the Father, Son, and Holy Spirit

Live Your Faith

God trusts humans to continually care for his creation. How do you take care of creation?

_____

_____

_____

_____

_____

_____

_____

_____

_____

_____

_____

_____

_____

_____

_____

_____

_____

Mini-Task

God's handiwork can be seen throughout all of creation.

God's work of creation is evident throughout all of salvation history. God's creation continues to unfold today, in both the big events of history and science and in the smallest functions of our lives and world.

Imagine you have been asked to create a ten-second video that zooms in on one aspect of God's creation that reveals him to you. What can you observe about God's unfolding creation on a micro level? Ideas include an ant building its home, a person hugging a friend, or a bee pollinating a plant.

Make a storyboard of your video. Write accompanying text that will be the narration for each still.

Choose a name for your video.

A

B

C

 Want to do more? Go to your Portfolio to continue this activity.

 **At Home**

The Church has a mission. Families have missions, too. Write out a mission statement for how your family wants to live.

Why did God make us?

Salvation history is God's saving work across time, leading us into eternity. God created us unlike any other creature, in his divine image and likeness, to live together and share in his life. From the beginning, our faith in God has been a part of his plan for us. Even when Adam and Eve turned away from God, God did not abandon his people. Through Jesus, all who have remained faithful to God will be welcomed into his Kingdom at the end of time.

Go to the digital portal for a prayer of intercession.

"God, who through the Word creates all things . . . gives men an enduring witness to Himself. . . . He ceaselessly kept the human race in his care . . . And in this manner prepared the way for the Gospel down through the centuries."

Dei Verbum, 3

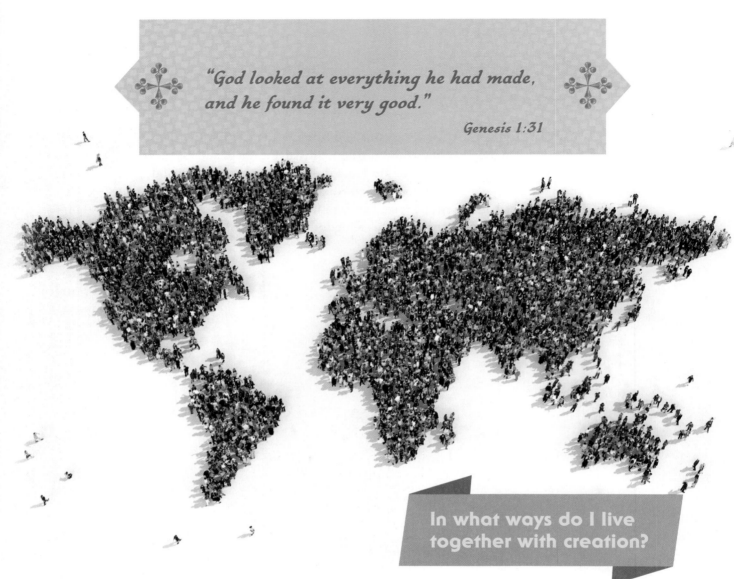

> *"God looked at everything he had made, and he found it very good."*
>
> *Genesis 1:31*

In what ways do I live together with creation?

We are created in God's image and likeness.

The world was created for the glory of God. All of creation comes from and shares in God's goodness. But only humans were created by God to share in his life.

We read in the first account of Creation that at the end of each day, "God saw that it was good" (see Genesis 1). Each of God's creatures shows us a particular aspect of his wisdom and goodness. God's creation is full of creatures that depend upon one another for their existence. Human beings, especially, were not created as solitary beings. Rather, we were made to live in loving community with one another. God created the first man and woman with equal human dignity. He created them to live in relationship with each other and with the Blessed Trinity.

Humans are the summit, or high point, of creation. We are the only part of God's creation called to share in God's own life. In fact, this is the very reason we were created.

Did You Know?

 Catholics need to be good stewards.

Faith is necessary for salvation.

God created us with the desire to know and love him. For this, God has given us the gift of faith. The New Testament Letter to the Hebrews defines faith as "the realization of what is hoped for and evidence of things not seen" (Hebrews 11:1). We are free to choose whether to accept the gift of faith. However, faith is necessary for our salvation. It enables us to believe in God and accept all that he has revealed to us.

In the Old Testament, we can read about our ancestors in faith. Of these ancestors, Abraham is one of the most important. He is a model of faith and obedience to the one, true God and to the truth. He responded with faith when God called him into a covenant relationship. By faith, he and his family went as strangers and pilgrims to the land God promised them. By faith, his wife, Sarah, would have a son in her old age. And because of his faith in God, Abraham was willing to offer that son as a sacrifice to God (see Genesis 12, 15, 22).

The Catechism of the Catholic Church tells us that our faith in God still "leads us to turn to him alone," the one, true God who is our beginning and "our ultimate goal" (*CCC*, 229).

Activity

Abraham is a model of faithfulness to God. He obeyed God in the most trying circumstances.

On the lines below, write about a time when you placed your trust in God during a difficult time. Write about how that made you feel. Share your story with a partner. Listen to your partner's story. Discuss how your stories are alike.

_____

_____

_____

_____

_____

Adam and Eve's choice to disobey God affects all humanity.

Chapter 3 of the Book of Genesis presents the account of Adam and Eve's choice to turn away from God. We call this event the Fall.

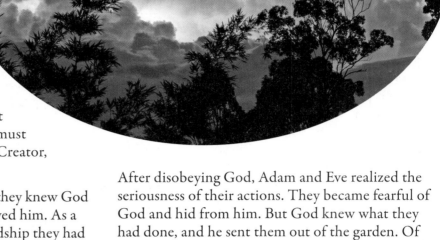

God gave Adam and Eve the Garden of Eden in which to live. They were free to do all but one thing: God forbade them from eating the fruit of the Tree of the Knowledge of Good and Evil. God told the man that if he ate from this tree, he would die. This warning symbolizes that friendship with God depends on complete trust in him and on following his will for us. It reminds us that as created beings, we must respect the limitations that God, our Creator, has established for us.

Adam and Eve freely chose to do what they knew God did not want them to do. They disobeyed him. As a result, they lost the harmony and friendship they had shared with God, with creation, and with each other. They became more likely to be guided by their bodily desires and emotions than by reason.

One Church, Many Cultures

In many cultures, stories are an important way to share our faith. Jesus told stories called parables to teach us about God the Father and his Kingdom. Jesus' stories used examples from everyday life that his listeners would understand. For example, the Parable of the Good Samaritan teaches that all people are our neighbor, to be treated with love (see Luke 10:25–37). In the Parable of the Sower, Jesus explained how people might respond to the Word of God. What stories could you tell to talk to others about your faith?

After disobeying God, Adam and Eve realized the seriousness of their actions. They became fearful of God and hid from him. But God knew what they had done, and he sent them out of the garden. Of their own free will, Adam and Eve chose to turn away from God.

The account of Adam and Eve shows how close the relationship between God and human beings originally was. It also shows that instead of trusting and obeying God, the first humans turned away from him and committed sin. A sin is a thought, word, deed, or action that goes against God's law. This sin of the first humans took away their original holiness and justice.

Adam and Eve's personal choice to turn from God was the first sin. It is called Original Sin. Original Sin weakened human nature and brought ignorance, suffering, and death into the world. This weakened human nature was passed on to the rest of humanity. We all suffer from the effects of Original Sin, even though we are not personally responsible for that sin.

Even after Adam and Eve turned away from God, God did not turn away from them. Instead, he showed them his mercy. He said a descendant of the first man and woman would save humanity (see Genesis 3:15). The Church calls this Scripture verse the *protoevangelium*, a Latin word meaning the "first gospel," because it is the first announcement of the Messiah and Redeemer.

Human nature was wounded by the sin of our first parents, but it was not destroyed. Humans were still a part of God's good creation, and God still loved them.

Activity

Imagine a modern-day story of Adam and Eve. Write a case study explaining how people today might turn away from God and what happened to them. Be sure to include an ending that shows God's mercy. Explain how the people in your study have returned to God's friendship. What lesson do you want your readers to take away from your story?

What Makes Us Catholic?

On All Souls' Day, November 2, the Church remembers in her prayers all those who have died. Many Catholics attend Mass on this day to pray for their deceased loved ones. We pray for them in the hope that God will welcome them into everlasting life with the Trinity. All Souls' Day reminds us not to be fearful of death, because Jesus' Resurrection means that we too can live with the hope of eternal life.

Read the Scripture account about the Garden of Eden and the Fall of Adam and Eve in Genesis 2–3.

Faith Words

hell see p. 257

Purgatory see p. 258

Last Judgment see p. 258

At the Last Judgment, Jesus Christ will judge all people.

God wants us to be with him, but we have the free will to choose to be close to him or not. How we choose to live here on earth will determine what happens when we die.

When we die, we will enter heaven, hell, or Purgatory. Even though we often think of it as a place, heaven is really a state of being in perfect friendship with God for all time. **Hell** is separation from God and from true happiness forever.

Many people who die in God's grace and friendship are not quite pure or holy enough to enter the joy of heaven. They may have committed venial sins, or they may have been attached to particular vices throughout their lives. These people may be sent to Purgatory before they are able to enter heaven. **Purgatory** demonstrates God's great mercy. It grants our soul an opportunity to be purged, or cleansed, of its attachments to sin so that we may dwell with God forever in heaven.

When we die, our souls will be separated from our bodies. However, God will reunite our bodies with our souls. Just as Christ is risen, so each of us will rise on the last day. At the **Last Judgment**, all people will be brought before Jesus Christ to give him an account of their actions. We will be judged by the way of life that Jesus describes: "whatever you did for one of these least brothers of mine, you did for me" (Matthew 25:40). The Corporal Works of Mercy come from this part of Matthew's Gospel.

Jesus tells us that when we care for others, we are serving him, too. When he comes again in glory at the end of time, Christ will judge us by our works and by how well we cooperated with God's grace. Those who have loved God and others will be welcomed into the Kingdom of God forever.

Partners in Faith

Saint Columba

Saint Columba lived nearly 1,500 years ago. Born in Ireland, he became a monk and a priest. He believed God's plan for him was to become a missionary. With twelve companions he traveled to Scotland in a wooden boat covered with leather. In addition to teaching the people of Scotland about Jesus, Saint Columba helped the fighting tribes make peace. He wrote hymns and transcribed nearly three hundred books. He died at the abbey he founded in Iona, Scotland.

 Learn more about the life of Saint Columba.

Faith Words

hell   **Purgatory**   **Last Judgment**

☑ Show What You Know

State whether each statement is true or false by circling the correct answer.
Correct any false statements.

1. Hell is the state of eternal separation from God.

   (True) | False

   _____

   _____

2. The period of time after a person dies, when he or she is purified—or becomes
   more holy before entering eternity with God—is known as Purgatory.

   (True) | False

   _____

   _____

3. Adam and Eve's personal choice to turn away from God is called original justice.

   True | (False)

   Orignal Sin

   _____

4. At the Last Judgment, Jesus will welcome all people into heaven.

   True | (False)

   Jesus will come at the end of time
   to judge all people

5. We are all created to share in God's life.

   True | False

   _____

   _____

Live Your Faith

You were created in God's image. How do you show God's image in
what you do and say?

_____

_____

How can you prepare for life in heaven while still on earth?

_____

Mini-Task

We pray for our friends and family members who have passed from this life into eternal life with Christ. One way to honor someone who has died is to tell that person's story.

Identify a friend, relative, saint, or holy person as the subject of a biography. Use the chart to write what you already know about the life of the person as well as what you want to learn. Then, write about what you learned.

Know		Want to know		Learned	
What do you already **know**?	Where did you get the information?	What do you **want to know** about this person?	Where can you find this information?	What did you **learn**?	How did you learn this information?

 Want to do more? Go to your Portfolio to continue this activity.

 At Home

Pray together for family members who have died, that they may live in eternal peace with God. Discuss how your family members can support one another in loving and serving God so that you, too, can live with him forever.

Who is Jesus Christ?

God's plan of salvation, in which we would come to share in his divine life, has been at work throughout all of salvation history. His plan came to completion in Jesus' Passion, Death, Resurrection, and Ascension. Jesus is the fulfillment of God's plan to save us from sin. His Resurrection makes possible our own resurrection.

 Go to the digital portal for a traditional prayer.

 "Save us, Savior of the world, for by your Cross and Resurrection you have set us free."

Roman Missal, The Mystery of Faith

Mary cooperated fully in God's plan of salvation.

Long ago, there lived a young woman named Mary in a town called Nazareth. Mary, who was a virgin, was engaged to a man named Joseph. One day, the angel Gabriel appeared to Mary. He greeted her with the words "Hail, favored one! The Lord is with you" (Luke 1:28).

At this event, called the Annunciation, Gabriel continued by saying: "Do not be afraid, Mary, for you have found favor with God. Behold, you will conceive in your womb and bear a son, and you shall name him Jesus. He will be great and will be called Son of the Most High, . . . and of his kingdom there will be no end" (Luke 1:30–33).

Mary asked the angel: "How can this be?" The angel replied: "The holy Spirit will come upon you, and the power of the Most High will overshadow you. Therefore the child to be born will be called holy, the Son of God" (Luke 1:35). Out of all women everywhere and at all times, God had chosen Mary to be the mother of his divine Son. God had been preparing Mary for this role in salvation history ever since the very moment of her conception in the body of her mother. Mary is unique among all people in that she was conceived without the stain of Original Sin. We call this the **Immaculate Conception**. Mary also remained pure from all personal sin throughout her life.

Faith Word

Immaculate Conception see p. 257

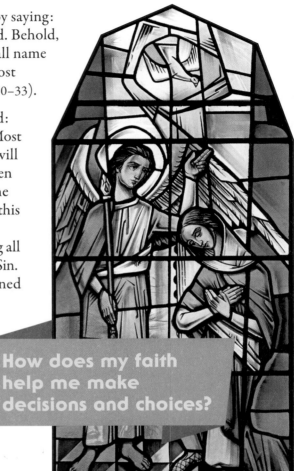

How does my faith help me make decisions and choices?

Did You Know?

Mary is with us today.

Activity

The first part of the Hail Mary prayer recalls the Annunciation. Explain in your own words what each line means.

Hail Mary _____

Full of grace _____

The Lord is with you _____

Blessed are you among women _____

And blessed is the fruit of your womb, Jesus _____

Now, tell the account of the Annunciation to a friend, using the words you wrote above. Then, pray the Hail Mary together.

In response to the angel's message, Mary had a decision to make. She could give in to fear and turn away from God's invitation. Instead, Mary said yes to God. She trusted God and knew that nothing was impossible for him. She replied to the angel: "Behold, I am the handmaid of the Lord. May it be done to me according to your word" (Luke 1:38).

Mary said "yes" to God's plan for her. She cooperated fully in God's divine plan of salvation. She is the Church's model of faith and holiness. Mary is the Mother of God, the Mother of the Church, and our mother. Everything about Mary's life, both her words and her actions, points us toward Jesus.

What Makes Us Catholic?

"Lamb of God" is a title for Jesus that you may be familiar with from the "Lamb of God" that you pray at Mass. This prayer is included in the *Roman Missal*, which contains all of the prayers for the celebration of the Mass. It also contains all the actions of the priest and the faithful, who are gathered to participate in the celebration of the Mass. We pray the Lamb of God during the Communion Rite to help us remember Jesus' sacrifice for our salvation.

In the Incarnation, Jesus, the Second Person of the Trinity, became man.

Faith Word

Incarnation see p. 257

The word *incarnation* means "becoming flesh." In the **Incarnation**, God the Son became flesh to save us from sin and reconcile us to the Trinity. Through the mystery of the Incarnation, Jesus, the Son of God, became man while remaining truly God. The Incarnation is a mystery we can only fully understand by faith. It reveals the depth of God's love for us.

Why did the Son of God need to become one of us? From the moment Adam and Eve sinned, humans have struggled to be faithful to God. But God never abandoned his people. He had a plan—the divine plan of salvation. He would send a Savior, his only Son, Jesus. Through his Passion, Death, Resurrection, and Ascension, Jesus saves us from sin and restores us to friendship with the Trinity.

The Incarnation is at the center of God's plan of salvation for humanity. The Word became flesh to save us from sin and to reconcile us to God. This means that Jesus Christ was both fully divine and fully human: true God and true man. Because of this absolutely unique identity, only Jesus could reconcile God and man. The Incarnation reveals the depth of God's love for us. Through Jesus, our model of holiness, we can participate in the very life of God.

> *"And the Word became flesh*
> *and made his dwelling among us,*
> *and we saw his glory,*
> *the glory as of the Father's only Son,*
> *full of grace and truth."*
>
> *John 1:14–15*

Activity

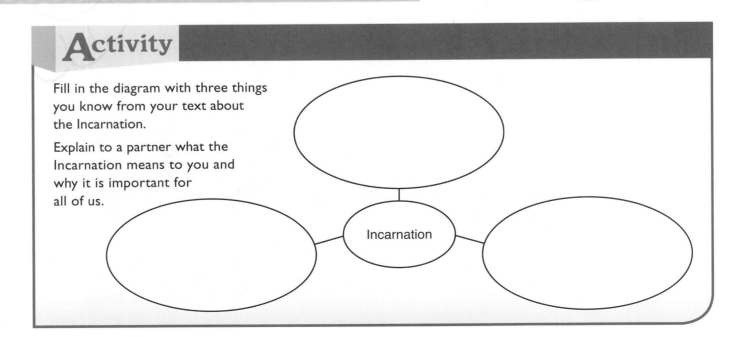

Fill in the diagram with three things you know from your text about the Incarnation.

Explain to a partner what the Incarnation means to you and why it is important for all of us.

Incarnation

"For just as through the disobedience of one person the many were made sinners, so through the obedience of one the many will be made righteous."

Romans 5:19

Jesus is the fulfillment of God's plan to save us from sin.

The Catholic faith is centered on Christ. Everything that we believe and celebrate has been revealed in him. "Christ" is the Greek translation of the Hebrew word *messiah*, which means "anointed one." Jesus was anointed for a special mission: he was the Savior God had promised his people. He would fulfill all of God's promises for salvation.

In the Old Testament, the prophet Isaiah described a servant of the Lord who would suffer greatly, not for his own sins but to save the people from theirs. Based on the preaching and teaching of Jesus, the early Christians understood Isaiah's words as a foreshadowing of the suffering and death of Jesus. Jesus freely gave his life for us, and in doing so, he freed us from our sins.

Jesus' Death and Resurrection are the fulfillment of God's plan to save humanity from sin. In the Apostles' Creed, we profess that Christ "descended into hell." This means that Jesus went into the realm of the dead. He opened the gates of heaven for all the just souls who had died before him and were awaiting his judgment. By experiencing real death, Jesus established his power over all of creation—over everything on earth, in heaven, and in hell. Because of Jesus' Resurrection, we can live with the hope that we too will have eternal life in heaven.

One Church, Many Cultures

Since the Church's earliest days and throughout the centuries, Jesus' followers have faced persecution for their faith. And since the Church's earliest days, Christians have been willing to suffer for their faith, some even to the point of death. Those who suffer and die for their faith are called martyrs. The first Christian martyr is Saint Stephen (see Acts of the Apostles 7:54–60). In many parts of the world today, Christians continue to be persecuted for being followers of Jesus. The Church prays that all her members and all people will be able to freely practice their faith and worship God.

Jesus' Resurrection provides hope for our own resurrection and eternal life with the Trinity.

The Resurrection and Ascension reveal the truth about Jesus, his teachings, and his mission. They make our own resurrection and eternal life with God possible.

Jesus appeared to the Apostles forty days after his Resurrection and reminded them of his promise to send the Holy Spirit. He reminded them of their mission to be his witnesses to the ends of the earth (see Acts of the Apostles 1:8).

Then suddenly Jesus was lifted up, and a cloud took him from their sight. The Acts of the Apostles describes the **Ascension** this way:

"While they were looking intently at the sky as he was going, suddenly two men dressed in white garments stood beside them. They said, 'Men of Galilee, why are you standing there looking at the sky? This Jesus who has been taken up from you into heaven will return in the same way as you have seen him going into heaven'" (Acts of the Apostles 1:10–11).

Jesus' Ascension into heaven assures us that we, too, can rise again, body and soul, at the end of time. With Jesus in heaven "seated at the right hand of the Father," we who are on earth continue his mission of announcing the Kingdom of God. We can do this without fear, because Jesus has given us the Holy Spirit to guide and strengthen us until the day when we are with him forever.

Faith Word

Ascension see p. 257

An illumination, or illustration, of the Ascension from a fifteenth-century prayer book

Partners in Faith

Saint Stephen

Saint Stephen was a deacon in the early Church. He made several prominent Jews angry because he taught that Jesus was the Son of God. They found him guilty of blasphemy and ordered him to be stoned to death. Saul (who later became the Apostle Paul) witnessed the death. Before he died, Stephen saw Jesus waiting for him in heaven. He said: "Behold, I see . . . the Son of Man standing at the right hand of God" (Acts of the Apostles 7:56).

 Learn more about the life of Saint Stephen.

Faith Words

Immaculate Conception
Incarnation   Ascension

Show What You Know

Complete the sentences.

1. Mary cooperated fully in God's divine plan of _____

2. The _____ is the event of Jesus' returning to the Father in heaven.

3. Jesus' Death and Resurrection are the _____ of God's plan.

4. The _____ is the teaching that from the very first moment of her life, Mary was free from Original Sin. She was full of God's grace.

5. Through the mystery of the _____ , Jesus, the Son of God, became man while remaining truly God.

Live Your Faith

Our mission is to announce the Kingdom of God. How can you do this?

_____
_____
_____
_____
_____
_____
_____
_____

How is Mary a model of holiness for you?

_____
_____
_____
_____
_____
_____
_____

How have I said yes to God?

Mini-Task

Mary's response to the angel Gabriel was a pivotal moment in God's plan of salvation.

In the space below, complete a story map about the Incarnation. Be sure to include key characters, events, and the outcome of those events, both immediately and today, in your life.

 Want to do more? Go to your Portfolio to continue this activity.

At Home

As a family, reflect on the meaning of the Incarnation. Invite family members to talk about how this mystery of our faith helps them understand who Jesus is.

What is the Church?

The Church was founded by Jesus Christ. The Church is the community of people who follow Christ and who love and serve him and the world. The Church goes out into the world to spread the Good News of salvation to all people. Under the leadership of the pope and bishops and with the guidance of the Holy Spirit, the Church continues her mission to bring all people to Christ.

Go to the digital portal for a prayer of petition.

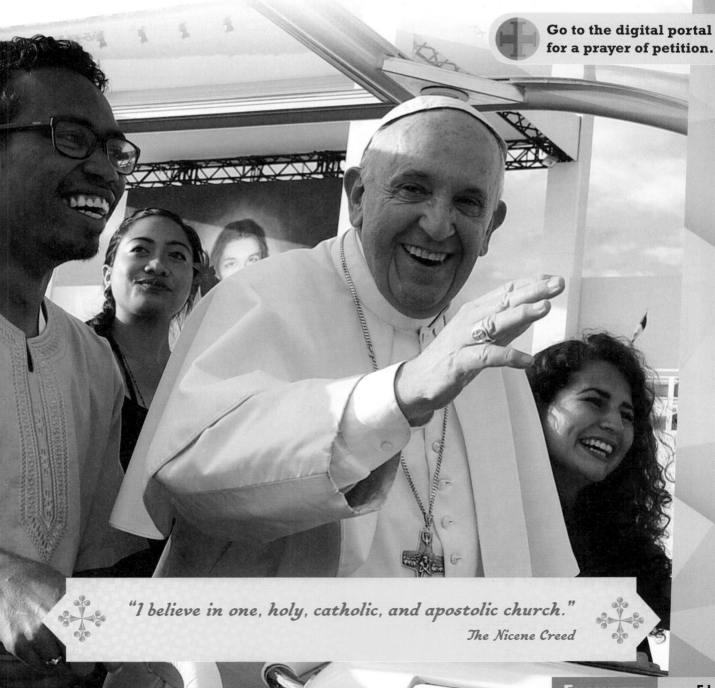

"I believe in one, holy, catholic, and apostolic church."
The Nicene Creed

The Church is human and divine.

The **marks of the Church** are that she is one, holy, catholic, and apostolic. As members of the Church, we are united as *one* in the beliefs that we profess. For example, we believe that we are all children of God who have been saved and made holy by God's loving plan. Perhaps most importantly, we are united in our belief in the Blessed Trinity: One God in Three Divine Persons. Indeed, the Church is one because God is one.

The human body is a miracle. Think about all of the different parts of the body and their functions. Each part is different from the next, yet all the parts work together. We humans don't say that we are made up of many different bodies. We are one physical body, with many parts that serve many functions for the whole body.

The *Catechism of the Catholic Church* explains this further by stating that our Church "acknowledges

Faith Word

marks of the Church
see p. 258

one Lord, confesses one faith, is born of one Baptism, forms only one Body, is given life by the one Spirit, for the sake of the one hope" (*CCC*, 866).

One symbol used to describe the unity of the Church is a body. Saint Paul expressed it this way: "As a body is one though it has many parts, and all the parts of the body, though many, are one body, so also Christ . . . . Now you are Christ's body, and individually parts of it" (1 Corinthians 12:12, 27).

Activity

The Church is the Body of Christ, carrying out Christ's work. Write one way people in your parish are doing Christ's work. Write one way you can do Christ's work this week.

_____

_____

_____

_____

When do I feel most united with other members of the Church?

Did You Know?

Catholics carry the Church with them.

The Church is one Body in Christ, both human and divine. The human reality of the Church is visible in her members, who are diverse and have many functions. We witness this reality when we walk into the sacred space of our church as well as when we gather for the Eucharist.

We experience the human reality through the teaching and service of the pope, bishops, and priests who lead the Church. We experience the human reality in our own families when we gather to pray and to celebrate God's presence with us.

The divine, or spiritual, reality of the Church can be harder to see. But, by faith, we can accept the mystery of the Church's invisible reality. Another image used to describe the Church that can help us to understand the Church's unity is the Bride of Christ. Just as a husband and wife are united as one in the Sacrament of Matrimony, so, too, are Christ and the Church deeply and fully one. In addition, this image reminds us that Christ loved the Church and gave himself to her.

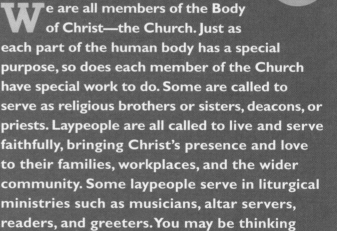

What Makes Us Catholic?

We are all members of the Body of Christ—the Church. Just as each part of the human body has a special purpose, so does each member of the Church have special work to do. Some are called to serve as religious brothers or sisters, deacons, or priests. Laypeople are all called to live and serve faithfully, bringing Christ's presence and love to their families, workplaces, and the wider community. Some laypeople serve in liturgical ministries such as musicians, altar servers, readers, and greeters. You may be thinking even now what your special work is. Pray that God will show you how to help your parish and community. Talk to people you trust who might help you understand how you can share your gifts to serve God and others.

All salvation comes from Christ through the Church.

The second mark of the Church is that she is *holy*. What does it mean to be holy? God calls us all to holiness, which means to be blessed with the presence and love of God. To be holy means to be one with God, united to the Blessed Trinity. It means to live a life that is on a path toward eternal life with God.

The Church is holy in a real and not yet perfect way. With the Holy Spirit guiding us, the members of the Church are always working to overcome sin and division and to be the holy People of God. All salvation comes from Christ, the Head, through his Body, the Church. In Christ, the Church is the sacrament of our salvation. Through the power of the Holy Spirit, the Church provides us what we need to attain eternal life. The Church encourages us on the path to holiness.

Some people, through no fault of their own, do not know Christ and his Church. Yet, the Church teaches that if people seek God with a sincere heart, with an openness to grace, and try in their actions to do God's will through listening to their consciences, they may achieve eternal salvation.

Activity

Imagine you are a reporter interviewing people about holiness. Ask two friends what they know about what it means to be holy. Write their answers on the lines. Now write a headline that will tell young people what it means to be holy.

_____

_____

_____

_____

_____

_____

_____

_____

_____

_____

_____

The Church has a missionary mandate to unite the whole world to Christ.

The third mark of the Church is "catholic." The word *catholic* means "universal." The Catholic Church's mission is to unite the whole world to Christ. The Church goes out to all people, everywhere. Guided by the Holy Spirit, the Church continues the mission of Christ. God "wills everyone to be saved and come to knowledge of the truth" (1 Timothy 2:4). The Church proclaims the fullness of faith and truth, and she is the means of salvation.

The Church's **missionary mandate** to go out to all people does not mean that we force people to believe as we do. Our task in proclaiming salvation is to enter into respectful dialogue with those who do not yet accept the Gospel. We benefit when we learn from them and appreciate the elements of truth and grace that are found among all peoples. The *Catechism of the Catholic Church* calls these elements "a secret presence of God" (*CCC*, 856).

Throughout salvation history, God has continually revealed himself to his people. In particular, he revealed himself to the Israelites, who later came to be known as Jews. They were his Chosen People, with whom he entered into a covenant that we call the Old Covenant. The Jewish faith, then, unlike other non-Christian religions, is a response to God's Revelation in the Old Covenant.

Faith Word

missionary mandate
see p. 258

The Jewish People are our ancestors in faith, and so the Catholic Church today has a profound love and respect for them. The Church rejects all forms of discrimination against Judaism and Jewish people. The Church also rejects anti-Semitic (anti-Jewish) teachings and ideas, including the misconception that the Jews are to blame for the death of Christ.

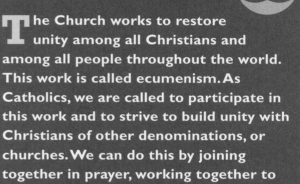

One Church, Many Cultures

The Church works to restore unity among all Christians and among all people throughout the world. This work is called ecumenism. As Catholics, we are called to participate in this work and to strive to build unity with Christians of other denominations, or churches. We can do this by joining together in prayer, working together to serve our communities, and supporting one another in our desire to do what God wills for us.

The pope and bishops succeed the Apostles.

Faith Word

apostolic succession
see p. 257

The fourth mark of the Church is "apostolic." How would the Good News of God's saving love be passed on from age to age? Recall Jesus' words to his Apostles to go "and make disciples of all nations, baptizing them in the name of the Father, and of the Son, and of the holy Spirit" (Matthew 28:19). Jesus founded the Church by giving his Apostles their mission: Go out into the world and tell everyone about God's truth and love.

We describe the Church as *apostolic* because the Apostles were empowered by the Holy Spirit to pass on the saving truths revealed by Christ. The earliest creed of the Church, the Apostles' Creed, summarizes these essential truths. Christ continues to lead the Church today, through the successors to the Apostles: the pope and bishops. This is called **apostolic succession**. It means that Christ gave the authority to act in his name to the Apostles, who gave it to their successors (bishops), who passed it on to *their* successors (more bishops), and so on, from generation to generation, all the way to the present day. Specifically, this authority is to sanctify, teach, and govern in the Church. It is passed on from one bishop to the next through the laying on of hands in the Sacrament of Holy Orders.

Christ entrusted Saint Peter with the "keys" to the Kingdom (see Matthew 16:15–19). The "keys" symbolize Saint Peter's authority and the idea that he would be the Church's visible leader after Christ's Ascension. The pope is the successor of the Apostle Peter. He is a caretaker of souls, "the Vicar of Christ and Pastor of the universal Church on earth" (*CCC*, 936). He is also the bishop of Rome.

Every bishop all around the world teaches the faith, celebrates the sacraments, and guides the Church. Each bishop is a "visible source and foundation of unity" (*CCC*, 938), both in the particular diocese that he leads and in the Church as a whole.

Partners in Faith

Saint Angela Merici

Saint Angela lived when many girls did not go to school. However, she strongly believed that an education would improve the lives of girls. Saint Angela and other women founded the Company of St. Ursula and began teaching poor girls. They taught the girls about God. They also taught them to read and write. Saint Angela said that God is always with us.

 Learn more about the life of Saint Angela Merici.

Faith Words

missionary mandate   **apostolic succession**
marks of the Church

 ## Show What You Know

Complete the sentences.

1. The Church proclaims the _____ of faith and truth.

2. The Church has a _____ to unite the world to Christ.

3. Through _____ , the authority Christ passed on to the Apostles is handed on to their successors, the bishops.

4. The _____ are that she is one, holy, catholic, and apostolic.

5. The Church is the _____ of our salvation.

Live Your Faith

Christ entrusted a mission to the Apostles: to go out into the world and proclaim the Good News of salvation. This is your job, too. Name three ways you can perform this job.

_____

_____

_____

_____

_____

_____

_____

_____

_____

_____

_____

_____

_____

_____

_____

_____

_____

Mini-Task

The ways we care for and treat other people should signal to the world that we are followers of Jesus.

Many young people today struggle with loneliness. How did Jesus treat people who were excluded? What can you do to help someone at school or in your community who is excluded and lonely?

Discuss a plan with a partner.

In the space below, describe specific steps you can take to reach out to and comfort someone in your school or community who may be excluded and feeling alone.

 Want to do more? Go to your Portfolio to continue this activity.

As a family, attend Mass celebrated by your bishop at your diocesan cathedral. If you are unable to travel, pray for your bishop and write him a letter of encouragement.

How do we celebrate what we believe?

Unit 2
The Faith Celebrated

The Great Commission

Unit Prayer

Leader: We learn from Saint Dominic that all that we have must be shared with others. We can start by sharing God's love with our families and friends. Then, we can learn to share with everyone we meet. We celebrate the love of God by sharing it with the world.

Let us listen to the stories of missionary disciples among us. They can tell us how to share and celebrate Jesus' love.

Leader: Let us pray:
Dear Jesus, help us to celebrate your love by sharing it with others.
Like Saint Dominic, we want to spread your love to everyone we meet.

Leader: Help us to make time for you in our busy lives.

All: Teach us to celebrate your love for us.

Leader: Help us to listen as you speak to us in the readings at Mass.

All: Teach us to celebrate your love for us.

Leader: Thank you for the gift of Holy Communion.

All: Teach us to celebrate your love for us.

Leader: Thank you for our families.

All: Teach us to celebrate your love for us.

(End the Unit Prayer by singing the song for this unit.)

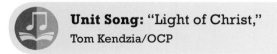

Unit Song: "Light of Christ,"
Tom Kendzia/OCP

Missionary Discipleship

How has someone in your family celebrated God's love with you? What happened? How did you feel?

How does God share his life with us?

God shares his life with us through the liturgy of the Church. The readings in the liturgy recount the events of salvation history. The Holy Spirit prepares us to encounter Christ in the liturgy and makes present the mystery of salvation. God entrusted the sacraments to the Church so that we could share in his life and grace. The Church also gives us sacred, or holy, signs called sacramentals to help us receive the grace of the sacraments.

Go to the digital portal for a *Lectio* and *Visio Divina* prayer.

"Holy Church celebrates the saving work of Christ on prescribed days in the course of the year with sacred remembrance. . . . throughout the course of the year the Church unfolds the entire mystery of Christ and observes the birthdays of saints."

Roman Missal, Universal Norms on the
Liturgical Year and Calendar, 1:1

Jesus leads his Body, the Church, in the liturgy.

One of the primary ways Catholics live their faith is through the celebration of the liturgy. In the liturgy, the Church celebrates the **Paschal Mystery**. The Paschal Mystery is Christ's Passion (or suffering), Death, Resurrection, and Ascension, through which he accomplished the work of our salvation. The Church proclaims and celebrates the Paschal Mystery so that we may receive the gift of salvation and the gift of God's grace. With these gifts, we bear witness to Christ in the world.

Liturgy is something we *do*. It is an action. But liturgy is not something we do alone, or even with just a few people. Liturgy is the public action of the "whole Christ," or, in Latin, *Christus totus*.

The "whole Christ" is the entire Body of Christ. This includes Jesus Christ as Head, and all the living baptized members of the Body, the Church. Christ also leads and celebrates for all time the heavenly liturgy with the Blessed Virgin Mary, the Apostles, the saints, and all those who have already entered God's Kingdom. They, too, are a part of the Body of Christ.

Christ, our redeemer and high priest, continues the work of redemption in, with, and through his Church. Liturgy is the work of Christ and the work of his Church. Every time we celebrate the liturgy, the communion in Christ between God and his People is manifested, or revealed. Liturgy engages us in the life of the Church. The Vatican II document *Sacrosanctum Concilium* explains that liturgy requires our "conscious, active, and fruitful participation" (*SC* 11, quoted in *CCC*, 1071).

Faith Word

Paschal Mystery see p. 258

Who has been a witness for me of Christ in the world?

Activity

The Church is at prayer all day, all around the world. On the clock below, write someone or something that you could pray for each hour. Now check the time. At this time of the day, pray for whomever or whatever you have listed.

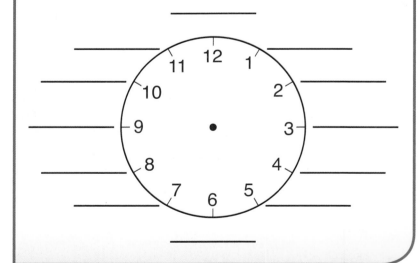

Did You Know?

There are many different types of liturgies.

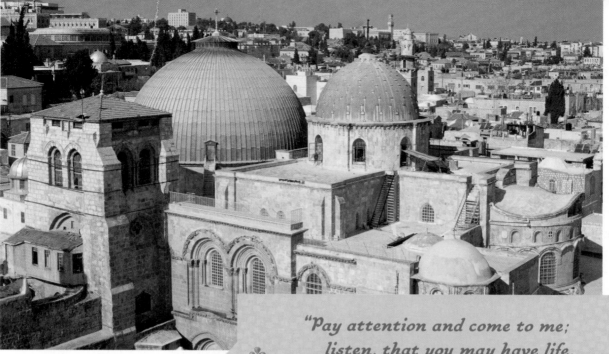

The site of the Church of the Holy Sepulchre in Jerusalem is identified as the place of both the crucifixion and the tomb of Jesus.

> *"Pay attention and come to me;*
> *listen, that you may have life.*
> *I will make with you an everlasting covenant,*
> *the steadfast loyalty promised to David."*
>
> Isaiah 55:3

The Holy Spirit prepares us to encounter Christ in the liturgy.

Throughout salvation history, the Holy Spirit was preparing the way for Christ and the Church. The gathering together of the People of God began when God called Abraham and promised that he would become the father of a great people. But Israel broke the covenant with God, and the prophets announced a New Covenant.

In the sacraments of the Church, the Holy Spirit fulfills what was foreshadowed in the Old Covenant. Even now, the Church's liturgy contains certain elements of worship from the Old Covenant, such as reading from the Old Testament and praying the Psalms. The Church's liturgy also recalls the saving events of salvation history now fulfilled in Christ. These include promise and covenant, Exodus and Passover, Kingdom and Temple, exile and return.

One Church, Many Cultures

The theme of exile and return can be felt strongly in the Catholic Church in China. After many years of forbidding the practice of Christianity, the Chinese government has allowed Catholicism to return as part of the Catholic Patriotic Association (CPA). However, the CPA is not in communion with Rome. So, for example, it appoints its own bishops rather than having bishops appointed by the pope. Chinese Catholics are split between the Catholic Patriotic Association and an "underground" church that is loyal to the Vatican. Many Catholic communities, especially in regions far away from major cities, practice the faith as it was taught by French missionaries in the nineteenth century and handed down to them. Chinese Catholics in these communities are rebuilding their churches and inviting others to live their faith.

The Holy Spirit had prepared the People of God for the messiah. The Holy Spirit, speaking through the prophets, tells us about Jesus Christ. The deeds, words, and symbols of the Old Covenant pointed the way to Christ. For example, the new life of Baptism is prefigured, or foretold, in the events of Noah and the flood (see Genesis 5–7) and the crossing of the Red Sea (see Exodus 14). Likewise, the manna God gave the Israelites to eat in the desert prefigures the Eucharist.

The Church relives the great events of salvation history in the liturgy. With the guidance of the Holy Spirit, the Church reveals the mystery of Christ that lies "hidden under the letter of the Old Testament" (*Catechism of the Catholic Church*, 1094). In every liturgy, the Church participates in the saving work of the Blessed Trinity. We praise and give thanks to God the Father, through God the Son, in God the Holy Spirit as we celebrate the Paschal Mystery.

"So Jesus said to them, 'Amen, amen, I say to you, it was not Moses who gave the bread from heaven; my Father gives you the true bread from heaven.'"

John 6:32

What Makes Us Catholic?

Images such as paintings, statues, and icons can encourage a deeper relationship with the mysteries of our faith. For example, Latin, or Roman Catholic, churches typically incorporate statues of Jesus, Mary, and the saints, while Eastern Catholic churches typically feature icons, a style of painted religious image. Religious works of art also serve to instruct. During the Middle Ages, when many people did not read or write, stained glass and other works of art in churches were designed specifically for the purpose of instructing the faithful. This artwork often depicted scenes from Scripture, especially from the Gospels, and events from the lives of the saints.

The sacraments are signs of grace entrusted to the Church by Christ.

Think about how Jesus Christ, who is the fulfillment of God's divine plan of salvation, preached, taught, and lived. He invited people to be adopted children of his Father. He forgave sinners, healed the sick, and blessed people. He brought strangers and even enemies together. He sent the Holy Spirit and commissioned his disciples to spread the Good News. In the Gospels, we discover how Jesus shared his life with those around him. But how would people continue to share in the life of the Trinity after Jesus died, rose, and ascended to heaven? In order that all people would be able to share in the Trinity's divine life forever, Jesus gave the Church the Seven Sacraments.

Through the power of the Holy Spirit, Christ in his Church uses the sacraments to confer particular graces. The sacraments make present the realities they signify through Jesus, who is at work in them. This means, for example, that in the Sacrament of Baptism, we *really and truly* become a new creation as a member of God's family, the Church. Or, in the Sacrament of Penance and Reconciliation, our sins are *really* forgiven. In and through all of the sacraments, we are invited to participate in God's life. Through the action of the Holy Spirit, we draw closer to Christ as we are invited to share in the life of the Blessed Trinity.

The most effective way that we can meet God is through the sacraments, particularly through the Eucharist. What do the sacraments do in us and for us? They call us to worship God and to build up the Church. The sacraments can deepen our faith if we are open to what God's love and grace can do in our lives. They guide us in how to pray, and they connect us to the Body of Christ, the Church. Most importantly, the sacraments sanctify us, or make us holy. With the power of the Spirit working in their lives, holy people can transform the world.

Sacraments communicate that God is present and among us. Through the sacraments, the Church continues to do what Jesus did.

Activity

Think about your parish church. On the lines below, write what you remember seeing as you walk in the door and look around. Compare your list with a partner. What did he or she remember that you did not?

At the entrance: ~~h~~ ~~water~~ opend doors

On the walls: noly water

Near the altar: bibles

In the pews: ~~neaters~~ kneelers

Statues: Jesus

Windows: tinted windoos

Other: _____

The next time you are at church, compare what you remembered with what is actually there.

Sacramentals prepare us to cooperate with the grace we receive in the sacraments.

What is one of the first things Catholics do when we enter church for Mass? First, we dip our fingertips in the font of holy water, which is in the vestibule, or the entrance to the church. Then we pray the Sign of the Cross. This action is a reminder of our Baptism. When we arrive at our pew, we either genuflect or bow in the direction of the altar and tabernacle. We enter the pew, and we may kneel in prayer. All of these actions—blessing ourselves with holy water, praying the Sign of the Cross, bowing, genuflecting, and kneeling—are **sacramentals**. The same is true of a statue of the Blessed Mother, statues or stained glass images of saints, a crucifix, and other sacred objects in church. These are sacramentals, too.

Sacramentals are sacred, or holy, signs that have been instituted by the Church. They prepare us to receive God's grace, especially in the sacraments. Sacramentals can be objects, such as blessed rosary beads, holy water, prayer cards, or statues. Sacramentals can also be certain devotions and prayers, such as the Rosary. Sacramentals can be certain actions, such as making the Sign of the Cross, bowing, genuflecting, or kneeling in prayer at home. The most important sacramentals are blessings. Both objects and people can be blessed. Not only is the blessing itself a sacramental, but what is blessed can also become a sacramental. Every blessing praises God for the many gifts he has given us. And, every blessing asks God to help us use these gifts according to the spirit of the Gospel.

Faith Word

sacramentals see p. 258

Partners in Faith

Saint Joan of Arc

Saint Joan of Arc is a national hero of France. She led the French army during the Hundred Years' War with England. When the English army captured her, they claimed she was a traitor and a heretic. After an unfair trial, she was burned at the stake in 1431. As she died, Saint Joan asked that a cross be held in front of her so she could see it. Joan attributed her bravery as a soldier to her faith in Jesus.

 Learn more about the life of Saint Joan of Arc.

Faith Words

sacramentals   **Paschal Mystery**

☑ Show What You Know

Complete the following sentences.

1. The liturgy recalls the events of _salvation_ history.

2. _liturgy_ is the work of Christ and his Church.

3. Jesus gave the Church the Seven _apostles_ so that all people would be able to share in God's divine life forever.

4. _sacramentals_ are sacred, or holy, signs that prepare us to receive God's grace, especially in the sacraments.

5. The _Paschal Mystery_ is Christ's Passion, Death, Resurrection, and Ascension.

Live Your Faith

What do the sacraments do for us?

_____

_____

_____

_____

_____

_____

_____

_____

_____

_____

What sacramentals have played important roles in your faith? In what ways?

_____

_____

_____

_____

_____

_____

_____

_____

Lesson 6
Portfolio

How can I participate more fully in the liturgy?

Mini-Task

The Church calls us to "active participation" at Mass. Active participation can include all of our senses and abilities.

This can mean engaging fully in the prayers and songs or listening intently to the Scripture readings and the homily. Active participation can also mean sharing our unique gifts and talents at Mass.

Fill in the Participation Survey below by listing your talents.

Participation Survey	
What are three ways that you actively participate at Mass?	
How does your active participation help you to grow in your faith?	
What can you do to inspire others to participate more actively at Mass?	

 Want to do more? Go to your Portfolio to continue this activity.

 At Home

Through the liturgy, our families meet Jesus and journey with God's people through the story of salvation history. With your family, think about each person's life story. When are some times when God has brought your family closer to him?

One of the main ways we praise and thank God is through celebrating and participating in the liturgy of the Church. The Church's liturgical year is filled with feasts and seasons and Sunday celebrations of the Lord's Day at Mass. This connects us to the life of Christ. Anywhere we might go in the world, the Church's liturgy celebrates the same Paschal Mystery. Devotions and forms of popular piety enrich our worship and help us live our faith.

Go to the digital portal for a prayer of meditation.

"Over the course of the year the Church celebrates the whole mystery of Christ, from the Incarnation to Pentecost Day and the days of waiting for the Advent of the Lord."

Roman Missal, Universal Norms on the Liturgical Year and Calendar, 1:17

We celebrate and participate in God's work through the liturgy.

"I'm going to work now!" This would be a strange thing to hear, or to say, on a Sunday morning when heading to Mass. Sunday, after all, is the "Lord's Day," the day of Christ's Resurrection. For this reason, it is the main day on which we celebrate the Eucharist. For many, it is a day of joy and rest from work, a time to be with family.

In a certain sense, however, saying "Let's go to work!" when heading to Mass is true. Why? When we participate in the liturgical celebrations of the Church, we are participating in "the work of God" and in God's work in us. Jesus spoke about this work when he said to his Father: "I glorified you on earth by accomplishing the work that you gave me to do" (John 17:4).

When the Body of Christ, the Church, celebrates liturgy, we gather to bless and praise God the Father, who is the source of all the blessings of creation. We worship and adore God, who offers us salvation, blesses us with his divine Son, and invites us to be his children.

Christ is present in the Church's liturgical celebrations, most especially when the Church celebrates the Eucharist at Mass. By the power of the Holy Spirit, Christ's mystery of salvation is made present. At Mass, we celebrate the Paschal Mystery: Christ's suffering, Death, Resurrection, and Ascension. Christ is present in his Word, in the person of the presider (priest or bishop), in the assembly gathered to pray and sing, and most especially in his Body and Blood. Through the Church's liturgy, we participate in God's saving work.

What do I do to participate in God's work during Mass?

Did You Know?

The Paschal Mystery is central to our Catholic faith.

The feasts and seasons of the liturgical year connect us to the life of Christ.

The Church year is based on the life of Christ and the celebration of his life in the liturgy. Because of this, the Church's year is called the **liturgical year**. The Church has its own way of marking the passing of time and the liturgical seasons of the year. Each season of the year stresses a different aspect of salvation history.

In one liturgical year, we recall and celebrate the whole life of Jesus Christ. We celebrate his birth, his younger years, his teaching and ministry, and, most importantly, his Paschal Mystery. During the year, we also venerate, or show devotion to, Mary, the Mother of God and all the saints. Keeping the memorials of the saints reminds us that we, the Church on earth, are united with the liturgy of heaven.

The liturgical year begins with the season of Advent in late November or early December, four Sundays before Christmas. The Sacred Paschal Triduum is the high point of the entire liturgical year, and the dates of all the other liturgical seasons are based upon the dates of the Easter Triduum. This is why the seasons begin and end at slightly different times each year.

Faith Word

liturgical year See p. 258

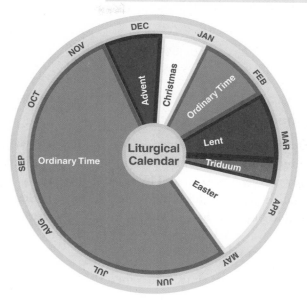

The order of Sunday readings in the Church's liturgy follows a three-year cycle. Each year is referred to by a letter: A, B, or C. This cyclical nature of the liturgical year means that, year after year, we are invited to enter ever more deeply into God's Word and the Gospel message. Year after year, the liturgy calls us to reflect on all of the themes of salvation history. These themes include Creation, Fall, Exodus, prophecy, Incarnation, forgiveness, healing, Death, Resurrection, Ascension, and discipleship.

Our faithful participation in the Church's liturgy, year after year, deepens our connection to the life of Christ. Each of the seasons of the Church year connects us more closely to Christ.

What Makes Us Catholic?

The Gospel readings during the Liturgy of the Word at Sunday Mass follow a three-year cycle. We mostly proclaim the Gospel of Matthew in Year A, the Gospel of Mark and one chapter of the Gospel of John in Year B, and the Gospel of Luke in Year C. The Gospel of John is read on certain Sundays of Lent and every year during the Easter season. The Scriptures are not necessarily read in the order they appear in the Bible, but they are connected to the feasts and seasons of the liturgical year. We can often find the readings listed in our parish missals or bulletins, or online at the United States Conference of Catholic Bishops (USCCB) Web site. These readings can help us prepare for next Sunday's Mass.

Activity

The liturgical year begins on the First Sunday of Advent and ends with the celebration of the Solemnity of Our Lord Jesus Christ, King of the Universe. In what season of the liturgical year does your birthday fall? Ask other members of your group about their birthdays. What seasons of the liturgical year contain their birthdays? Talk about how your birthday celebrations can be enriched by the liturgical seasons.

> *"Go, therefore, and make disciples of all nations, baptizing them in the name of the Father, and of the Son, and of the holy Spirit."*
>
> *Matthew 28:19*

Apostolic Tradition unifies the different celebrations in the worldwide Church.

After the Spirit had descended on the Apostles at Pentecost, they began to spread the Gospel message. They traveled by land and by sea. Saint Peter established the Church in Rome. Other Apostles traveled beyond the Roman Empire. Soon, the Church was celebrating liturgy in places far beyond Jerusalem.

All the way across time, from when the first Christian community in Jerusalem celebrated the liturgy until now, the Church continues to celebrate the same Paschal Mystery. This means that no matter where in the world you go to Mass, you are celebrating the same saving events. In a different part of the world from your own, however, you would likely experience unique cultural expressions reflected in the liturgy.

Catholics celebrate Mass in Lahore, Pakistan.

Catholics celebrate Mass in Brazzaville, Republic of the Congo.

The *Catechism of the Catholic Church* explains the diversity of expression in this way:

"Through the liturgical life of a local church, Christ, the light and salvation of all peoples, is made manifest to the particular people and culture to which that Church is sent and in which she is rooted. The Church is catholic, capable of integrating into her unity, while purifying them, all the authentic riches of cultures" (*CCC*, 1202).

Notice that Jesus did not tell his Apostles: "Go out to one or two nations, make a few disciples, and baptize them." Rather, the Apostles were told to go out to all nations. So, all the different ways of celebrating the liturgy in the worldwide Church rest upon the same foundation: Apostolic Tradition, the faith of the Apostles. The Church is catholic, universal—for all people and all nations.

One Church, Many Cultures

Before Christmas in Latin America and some parishes in the United States, Catholics participate in a nine-day devotion called *Las Posadas. Las Posadas* remembers the journey of Mary and Joseph just before Jesus' birth. A man and woman dress up as Joseph and Mary and lead a procession to a different house that represents a posada, or inn, every night for eight nights. They pray in front of a Nativity scene. Then carols are sung and children break open a piñata shaped like a star, to represent the Star of Bethlehem. A similar celebration, called *Simbang Gabi*, is held in the Philippines.

Devotions enrich our faith and prepare us to celebrate the sacraments.

We encounter God in the liturgy of the Church, particularly in the sacraments. We encounter God through sacramentals, which are holy signs that prepare us to receive God's grace. We also encounter God through **devotions**, a form of personal prayer, and other forms of popular piety or communal expressions of faith.

Devotions and forms of popular piety can bring us closer to Jesus. They can help us pray. They can help us both to live the Good News and to share it with others.

Popular devotions enrich our prayer and help us live our faith. Here are a few of them:

- Stations of the Cross
- pilgrimages to holy places
- lighting candles in the church
- processions on feast days
- wearing holy medals
- devotions to the Sacred Heart of Jesus, Divine Mercy of Jesus, and the Blessed Mother

Faith Word

devotions see p. 257

Activity

Many churches have the Stations of the Cross on the walls. These are fourteen images reminding us of Christ's Passion and Death. (Refer to the Stations of the Cross on page 246 of this book.) Discuss one of the questions below with your group. Report your conclusions to the entire group.

- What would have happened if Pilate had not condemn Jesus?
- Why do you think Jesus fell three times?
- What might have happened if Simon had not helped carry the cross?
- What do you think the women wanted to do for Jesus?

Partners in Faith

Saint Leonard of Port Maurice

Saint Leonard of Port Maurice was a great preacher. He spent over forty years preaching, especially during Lent. He gave special attention to the "Way of the Cross," the path Christ took to his death on the Cross. Saint Leonard set up Stations of the Cross all over Italy for people who could not travel to the Holy Land. Today, many churches have Stations of the Cross on their walls so the faithful can symbolically walk to Calvary with Jesus.

Learn more about the life of Saint Leonard of Port Maurice.

Faith Words

liturgical year **devotions**

 ## Show What You Know

Circle the correct term to complete each sentence.

1. Holy signs that prepare us to receive God's grace are called _____ .
   a. devotions
   b. sacramentals
   c. symbols

2. _____ are forms of personal or communal prayer.
   a. Devotions
   b. Sacramentals
   c. Feasts

3. The liturgical year is the calendar of the liturgies and _____ of the Church.
   a. gifts
   b. laws
   c. prayer

4. Which of these is **not** a devotion?
   a. the Rosary
   b. the Eucharist
   c. the Stations of the Cross

Live Your Faith

What differences do you think you might see or hear at Mass in another country?

_____

_____

_____

_____

_____

What kinds of devotions have you participated in? Which devotions would you like to try?

_____

_____

_____

_____

_____

_____

How do I live out the liturgical year?

Mini-Task

The Church's liturgical year starts on the first Sunday of Advent. On the secular calendar, this is in late November or early December. While the rest of our society celebrates the new year on January 1, the Church year begins by anticipating the birth of Jesus Christ, who is known as Emmanuel, God-with-us.

Think about the liturgical year. What three liturgical seasons celebrated in your parish do you notice the most? Write the three seasons you have identified in the chart. Then write one way you can better live out the meaning of each of these seasons this year.

Season of the liturgical year	How I will live out the meaning of the season

 Want to do more? Go to your Portfolio to continue this activity.

Look at your family calendar, or a calendar you have in your room. Do some research, and with your family, mark the Church's special feasts and seasons on the calendar. Plan to celebrate the seasons with your entire family.

How do we become members of the Church?

The Sacraments of Christian Initiation make us members of Christ's Body, the Church. The grace we receive in these sacraments strengthens us to live as faithful disciples. The grace of Baptism calls us to share in Christ's work as priest, prophet, and king. The Sacrament of Confirmation seals us with the Gift of the Holy Spirit and perfects the grace of Baptism. The Eucharist nourishes us with Christ's Body and Blood and unites us to his life, saving work, Death, and Resurrection.

 Go to the digital portal for a prayer of petition.

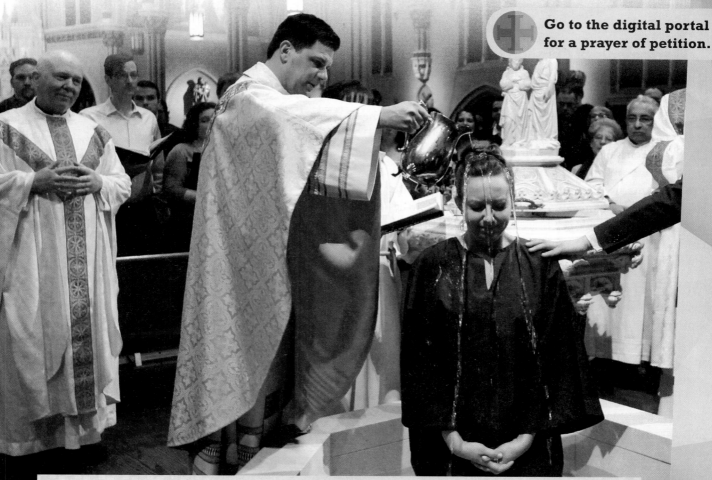

"Father,
through your holy prophets
you proclaimed to all who draw near you,
'Wash and be cleansed,'
and through Christ you have granted us rebirth in the Spirit."

Rite of Christian Initiation of Adults

Faith Word

Sacraments of Christian Initiation see p. 258

The Sacraments of Christian Initiation are the foundation of the Christian life.

Jesus gave the Church an amazing treasure: the treasure of divine life. Through the Seven Sacraments, he gave us the means to grow in love and participate in the divine life of God. The Sacraments of Baptism, Confirmation, and Eucharist are the three **Sacraments of Christian Initiation**. These three sacraments introduce us into the Christian life. They initiate new members into the Body of Christ, the Church. When we celebrate these sacraments, we remember and enter into the Paschal Mystery of Jesus and celebrate God's presence among us today.

The Sacrament of Baptism is the first Sacrament of Christian Initiation. It is essential for salvation. The baptized person dies to sin and rises to new life in Christ. Baptism imprints a permanent spiritual sign on a person's soul. This is why Baptism can only be celebrated once in a person's life. The Sacrament of Confirmation perfects the grace of Baptism and also imprints a permanent spiritual mark on the soul. The anointing with sacred chrism, the laying on of hands by the presider, and the words of the sacrament impart the fullness of the Holy Spirit on the candidate. In the Sacrament of the Eucharist, the baptized share in the Body and Blood of Christ and are nourished to live as his faithful disciples.

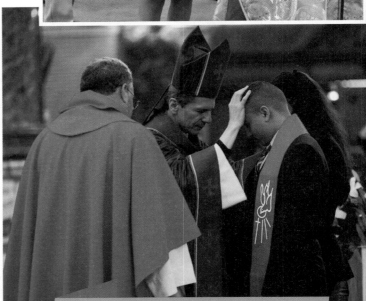

What makes me a disciple of Jesus Christ?

Did You Know?

Catholic disciples continue to renew the Church.

The grace we receive in Baptism calls us to share in Christ's work as priest, prophet, and king.

We learn from the Old Testament that being anointed with holy oil set a person apart to serve God as a king, a priest, or a prophet. At Jesus' baptism in the Jordan River, the Holy Spirit came upon him and revealed him to be the Father's beloved Son. His baptism also revealed Jesus to be the Christ, or "anointed one," who is priest, prophet, and king. We call Jesus a priest because he gave the sacrifice that no one else could. He offered himself to save us. Jesus was a prophet because he delivered God the Father's message of love and forgiveness and called people to faith. He also spoke out for truth and justice. Jesus showed himself to be a king by the love and care he gave to all his people.

Anointing is important in the life of the Church today. In the Church's sacraments, to be anointed with oil signifies the power of the Holy Spirit being poured out on the person receiving the sacrament. In Baptism, we are anointed with Sacred Chrism and marked forever as belonging to Christ. As a member of Christ's Body, we are called to share in his work as priest, prophet, and king.

• *Through Baptism, we share in Jesus Christ's work as priest.* Our participation in Christ's priesthood is called the **common priesthood of the faithful**. Everything we do—our work, play, studying and learning, prayer, participation in the liturgy (particularly the Eucharist), activities with family and friends, and even the hard times that are part of life—becomes a spiritual offering to God when we unite it to the sacrifice of Christ.

Faith Word

common priesthood of the faithful see p. 257

Isaiah 61:1–3
You have anointed me.

Pilgrims to World Youth Day in Poland are reminded of the way they are connected to the Church in the common priesthood of the faithful.

One Church, Many Cultures

While the Latin, or Roman, Catholic Church shares the same beliefs and most rituals with the Eastern Catholic Churches, one difference is in the type of bread used in the Sacrament of the Eucharist. In the Roman Catholic Church, only unleavened bread, or bread made without rising ingredients such as yeast, can be used in the sacrament. This connects us to the Last Supper, because the bread Jesus broke with his disciples was also unleavened. In contrast, the Eastern Churches use leavened bread containing yeast. This choice connects the Eastern Churches with traditions that use yeast to symbolize the soul that gives life to the body.

- *Through Baptism, we share in Jesus Christ's work as prophet.* We are called to be prophets like the Old Testament prophets, like John the Baptist, and like Christ himself. A **prophet** is someone who speaks on behalf of God, reminds people to be faithful to God, defends the truth, and works for justice. Saint Francis of Assisi wrote in his Testament: "the Most High Himself revealed to me that I should live according to the form of the holy Gospel." We are all called to live according to the Gospel, to spread the Good News of salvation, and to bear witness to God's Word wherever we are. In all of these ways we can help lead others to God.

- *Through Baptism, we share in Jesus Christ's work as king.* Jesus Christ was a king who served others. John the Baptist said of Jesus: "Behold, the Lamb of God, who takes away the sin of the world" (John 1:29). Jesus' mission was to serve and to give himself so that we might have life. His reign makes the love of the Trinity present and active in the world. We follow Jesus' example and offer ourselves to others in loving service. We witness to God's kingdom of love, justice, and mercy.

In Baptism:

- Original Sin and personal sins are forgiven.
- We become children of God, new creations. Our new relationship with God is sealed with a permanent spiritual mark.
- We begin our new life in Christ as members of his Church, the Body of Christ.
- We are united with other Christians.

Faith Word

prophet see p. 258

Activity

Through our Baptism, we share in Christ's work as priest, prophet, and king. Think about what each of these means to you and how you can carry out these in your life. Share with a partner one way you can carry out this work this week.

- Through Baptism, we share in Christ's work as priest.

_____

- Through Baptism, we share in Christ's work as prophet.

_____

- Through Baptism, we share in Christ's kingly mission.

_____

What Makes Us Catholic?

The Church celebrates Christ's kingship all year long, but most especially on the Solemnity of Christ the King. This Solemnity is the last Sunday of the liturgical year, before the new year begins on the first Sunday of Advent. This day is the final Sunday of our liturgical year and of the season of Ordinary Time. It honors Christ as Messiah and as the King of Kings, who reigns over all of heaven and earth, and holds dominion over sin, suffering, and death. We can honor Christ as King each day by following his example and trusting his authority.

Faith Word

Confirmation see p. 257

Confirmation perfects baptismal grace.

All baptized members of the Church should receive the **Sacrament of Confirmation**. Confirmation perfects the grace we first received at Baptism. Like Baptism, it imprints on our souls a character, a permanent spiritual seal. This is why we receive this sacrament only once.

In Confirmation:

- We are sealed with the Gift of the Holy Spirit.
- We become more like Jesus and are strengthened to be his witnesses.
- We deepen our relationship with God the Father.
- Our bond with the Church is strengthened.
- We are sent forth to live our faith in the world.

In the Sacrament of Confirmation, the Holy Spirit gives candidates the strength to take on the responsibilities of being disciples of Christ who share in his mission as fully initiated members of his Church. The Holy Spirit guides them to love and serve Jesus always.

When we receive the Sacrament of Confirmation, the Holy Spirit gives us special gifts. During the Rite of Confirmation, the presider (usually a bishop) extends his hands over the candidates. He prays:

"Give them the spirit of wisdom and understanding, the spirit of counsel and fortitude, the spirit of knowledge and piety; fill them with the spirit of the fear of the Lord" (*The Order of Confirmation*, 25).

These seven gifts of the Holy Spirit help us to live as faithful followers of Jesus Christ.

Activity

Think of as many words or phrases as you can that refer to Confirmation, such as *Gift of the Spirit* and *sealed*. Write down these words and phrases. Choose one word or phrase, and share with a friend why that word or phrase is particularly meaningful to you.

_____

_____

_____

_____

_____

> "Then he took the bread, said the blessing, broke it, and gave it to them, saying, 'This is my body, which will be given for you; do this in memory of me.' And likewise the cup after they had eaten, saying, 'This cup is the new covenant in my blood, which will be shed for you.'"
>
> Luke 22:19–20

The Eucharist unites us to the Paschal Mystery.

We read in the Old Testament that God made a covenant with Moses and his people. Jewish people today still live by this covenant. Every year, they gather to celebrate a feast called Passover. They remember the miraculous way that God saved them from death and slavery in ancient Egypt. The angel of God "passed over" the houses of his people, protecting them from the suffering that came to the Egyptians.

On the night before Jesus died, he and the Apostles celebrated Passover in Jerusalem. During this meal, Jesus gave his disciples a special way to remember him and to be with him. At the Last Supper, Jesus gave us the gift of himself by instituting the Eucharist.

Jesus' Death and Resurrection established a new and everlasting Covenant. Through this New Covenant Original Sin and personal sins are forgiven. We are made sons and daughters of God by grace and adoption. We are justified by grace and called to share in God's divine life. In the Sacrament of the Eucharist, we celebrate and receive Jesus Christ, who offered his Body and Blood as a sacrifice to establish the New Covenant. By the power of the Holy Spirit, the Paschal Mystery of Christ's suffering, Death, Resurrection, and Ascension is made present again. Jesus is truly present under the appearances of bread and wine. When we receive the Body and Blood of Christ in Holy Communion, we are united with Christ's saving work. Through the Eucharist, Jesus remains with us forever.

In the Eucharist:

- We are nourished by the Word of God and receive Jesus Christ in Holy Communion.
- We are joined more closely to Christ and one another.
- Grace, the life of God which we first received in Baptism, deepens in us.
- We are strengthened to love and serve others.
- We receive a foretaste of the Kingdom of heaven.

Partners in Faith

Saint Charles Lwanga

Saint Charles Lwanga lived in Uganda, where he served as a page to the king of Buganda. The king disliked Christians and ordered Charles and his friends to do immoral things. When Charles would not obey, the king demanded that he renounce his Catholic faith. Charles refused, and the king ordered him to be burned alive. Charles and twenty-one other Christian men and boys were killed together.

 Learn more about the life of Saint Charles Lwanga

Faith Words

Sacraments of Christian Initiation
common priesthood of the faithful
prophet   Confirmation

 Show What You Know

Explain each term in your own words.

1. Confirmation

_____

_____

_____

2. common priesthood of the faithful

We s Are m chrst preist here
through da sacrement and confirmer

_____

3. Sacraments of Christian Initiation

_____

_____

_____

4. prophet

_____

_____

_____

Live Your Faith

How do you share in Christ's work as priest, prophet, and king?

_____

_____

_____

_____

_____

_____

_____

How am I a prophet?

Mini-Task

In the Old Testament, the prophets' role was to keep the leaders and people of the time faithful to God's covenant. They did this through the clothes they wore, the food they ate, and the words they said (or did not say). Through our Baptism, we share in Christ's ministry as prophet. We are called to live our faith and to be Christ's witnesses in the world.

Write a graphic novel about a situation in which a modern-day prophet is calling people to be faithful to Christ. What wrong or injustice is the prophet pointing out to his or her audience? What media is the prophet using to broadcast his or her message? What is the response?

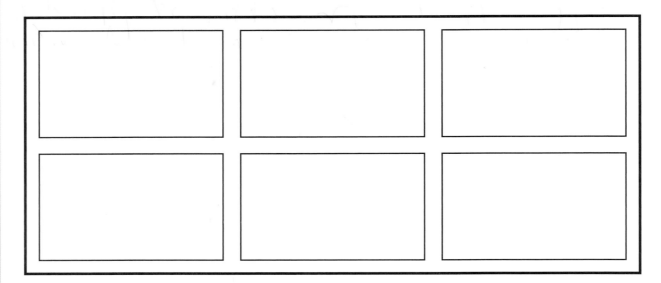

 Want to do more? Go to your Portfolio to continue this activity.

When you were baptized, you were anointed with Sacred Chrism, which is special, perfumed oil blessed by the bishop. God called you to be a "priest, prophet, and king." Talk with your family about what these words mean for a baptized Christian. Think about your everyday life. What opportunities do you see for you to be a priest, prophet, and king?

How do we celebrate God's forgiveness and healing?

During his ministry, Jesus taught his followers about God's love and forgiveness. He healed those who were sick, and he forgave sins. The Church continues Jesus' saving work in a special way through two Sacraments of Healing: Penance and Reconciliation and Anointing of the Sick. These sacraments restore our relationship with God and the Church; invite us to conversion; forgive our sins; and bring us peace, courage, and strength.

Go to the digital portal for a prayer of praise.

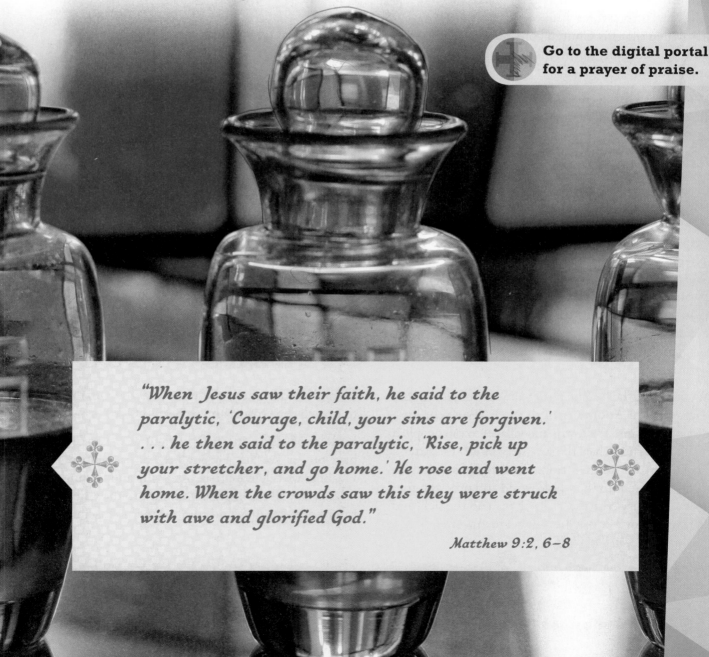

"When Jesus saw their faith, he said to the paralytic, 'Courage, child, your sins are forgiven.' . . . he then said to the paralytic, 'Rise, pick up your stretcher, and go home.' He rose and went home. When the crowds saw this they were struck with awe and glorified God."

Matthew 9:2, 6–8

The Sacraments of Healing celebrate God's forgiveness and mercy.

Jesus gave the Church the **Sacraments of Healing**: the Sacrament of Penance and Reconciliation and the Sacrament of Anointing of the Sick.

Christ, the physician of body and soul, through the power of the Holy Spirit, heals our souls and gives us peace, courage, and strength to endure illness through these Sacraments of Healing. *The Catechism of the Catholic Church* explains:

"The Lord Jesus Christ, physician of our souls and our bodies, who forgave the sins of the paralytic and restored him to bodily health, has willed that his Church continue, in the power of the Holy Spirit, his work of healing and salvation" (*CCC*, 1421).

We first receive forgiveness of sin in Baptism. We are washed clean of the stain of Original Sin and of all personal sins and we begin a new life in Christ. Yet, after Baptism, we sometimes turn away from God. We are always in need of his forgiveness. The Church celebrates God's forgiveness in the Sacrament of Penance. In this sacrament, our relationship with God and the Church is restored, and our sins are forgiven. There is a strong connection between the Sacraments of Baptism and of Penance. Baptism creates us anew as children of God and members of the Church. Penance restores our relationship with God and the Church when it has been harmed or broken by our sin.

Faith Word

Sacraments of Healing
see p. 259

When have I witnessed God's forgiveness and healing at work in the world?

We celebrate the healing power and love of Jesus in the Sacrament of Anointing of the Sick. Jesus sent his disciples out into the towns and villages to call people to repentance and to heal the sick (see Mark 6:7–13). After his Death and Resurrection, Jesus commissioned his disciples: "Go into the whole world and proclaim the gospel to every creature. . . . lay hands on the sick, and they will recover" (Mark 16:14, 18). The Apostles, strengthened by the Holy Spirit, went out into the world to preach the Gospel and to heal in Christ's name.

Because of Jesus, sin, suffering and death no longer have power over us. Through the Sacraments of Healing, we celebrate Jesus' forgiving and healing love. To this day, all the baptized can turn to the Church for forgiveness, healing, and comfort in these sacraments.

Did You Know?

Metanoia **is the Greek word for conversion.**

The Sacrament of Penance and Reconciliation invites us to respond to Jesus' call to conversion.

Sometimes we don't live the life God wants for us—a life of communion with him and others. Because of human weakness, we turn away from God and we sin. God's desire is that we share in his life. Even when we sin, God never stops loving us. He never stops reaching out to us with his divine mercy. God continues to invite us to himself.

Accounts of God's mercy fill the Old Testament. God is always reaching out to his people, calling them back to their covenant relationship with him. No one is beyond the reach of God's mercy. Psalm 51 is a beautiful, heartfelt prayer of repentance in which the psalmist turns back to God with total trust in his mercy and forgiveness.

In the Gospels, Jesus helped others turn away from sin and toward God the Father. Jesus often taught his followers to show their love for God by loving and forgiving others. In the Parable of the Prodigal Son,

Faith Word

conversion See p. 257

Jesus helps us understand what it means to be sorry for our sinful actions and turn back to God (see Luke 15:11–24). God is like the forgiving father in this story. He welcomes us back with unconditional love and rejoices when, through his grace, we decide to return to him.

God constantly calls us to **conversion**. Conversion is a turning to God with all one's heart. If we trust God, he will show us how to change and grow into the people he wants us to be. Conversion is the work of God's grace within us. It happens over and over again. It leads us to live in a way that is pleasing to God, according to his love. The Holy Spirit gives us this desire to change and grow. With the support of the Church, especially the healing mercy that is always available to us in the Sacrament of Penance and Reconciliation, we can respond to God's call every day.

What Makes Us Catholic?

As Catholics, we can look to the example of several saints who experienced conversion. Some of the Church's most honored saints directed their lives away from God until they eventually accepted God's invitation to himself. Saints Paul, Ignatius of Loyola, Augustine of Hippo, and Thomas Becket all had powerful conversion experiences either while struggling physically or emotionally, or in a moment of unexpected connection to Christ. Our own experience of conversion leads us to a deeper relationship with God and the Church. It also gives us the chance to share—with others who may be struggling with their faith—what we have learned and felt.

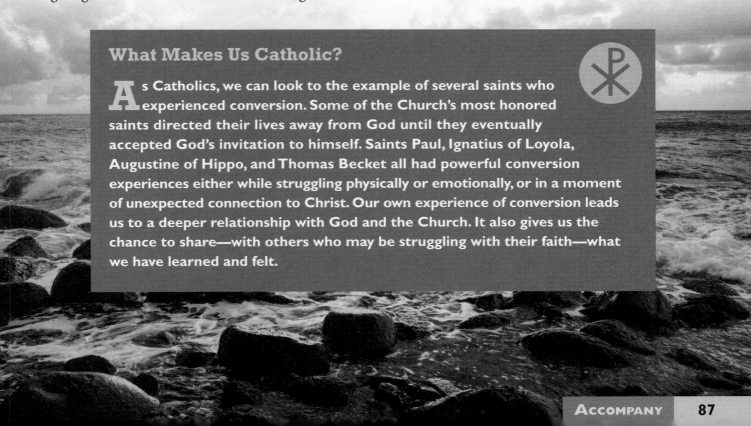

The Sacrament of Penance and Reconciliation reconciles us with God and the Church.

All of the sacraments bring us closer to God and unite us more fully with believers everywhere. Through the Sacrament of Penance and Reconciliation in particular, we are reconciled with God and restored to God's grace.

To celebrate the Sacrament of Penance, we must first be truly sorry for our sins and firmly intend not to sin in the future. This is called repentance, or contrition. Then, we must confess our sins to a priest. After hearing our confession, the priest will propose some action we can take to repair, at least partially, the harm our sins have caused. This is called an act of penance. We are responsible for carrying out the penance the priest has given us. Lastly, the priest prays the prayer of absolution, declaring that our sins have been forgiven. It is the priest's authority, given by the Church, that enables him to forgive sins in the name of Christ.

As one Body of Christ, the whole Church benefits from our just and loving actions. Because the whole Church also suffers when one person turns away from God, the reconciliation of one member of the Church with God strengthens all of us.

Activity

Fill in the diagram, showing how a just or loving action benefits the whole Church. In the center of the diagram, write the action. Fill in the outer circles with the effects of that action on the Church.

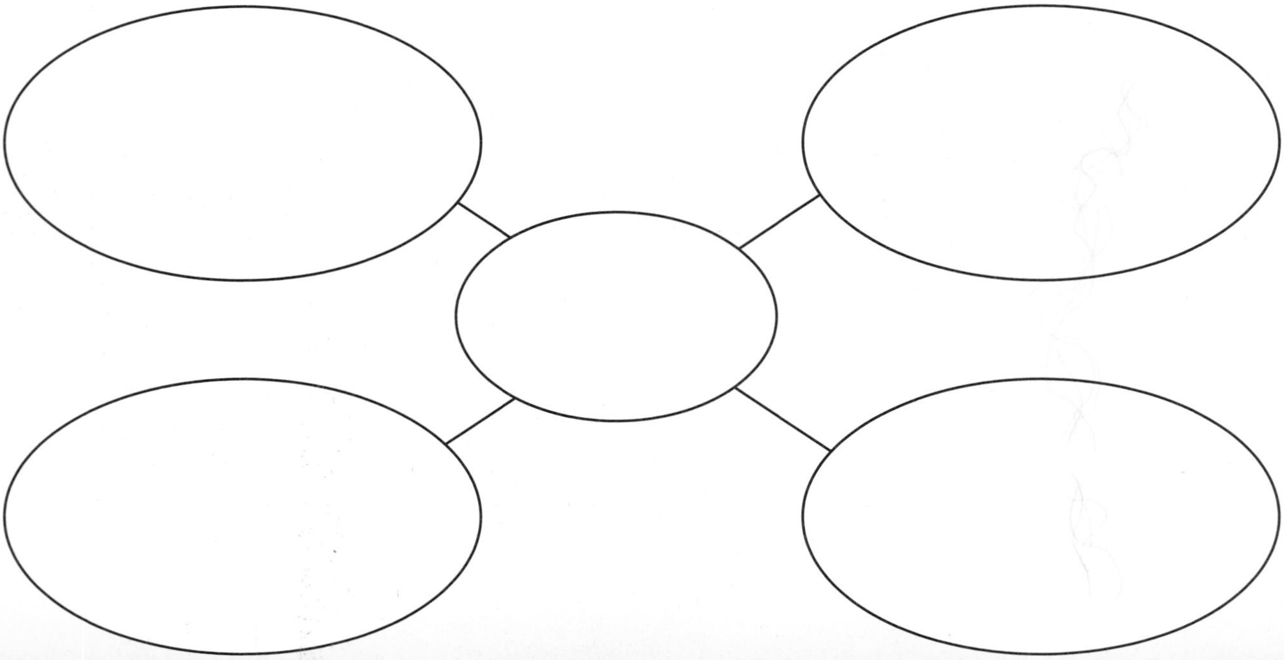

In the Sacrament of Penance, we are forgiven. We are also called to forgive others always. When we forgive others, we grow as a loving and reconciling community. Reconciliation with God and the Church contributes to peace and reconciliation in the world. We are better able to stand up for what is right and to act with justice. We experience the peace that comes from knowing that our relationship with God has been restored.

The grace of the Sacrament of Penance and Reconciliation

- forgives our sins
- reconciles us with God
- reconciles us with the Church
- gives our conscience peace and consolation
- strengthens us to live by the Ten Commandments and by Jesus' teaching.

One Church, Many Cultures

The Church takes all forms of the work of healing seriously. Many Catholic doctors, nurses, and others in the medical field participate in medical mission work for and with the worldwide Church. Organizations such as Catholic Relief Services join local groups to promote nutrition, health care, and good hygiene, especially in areas in which people are suffering from natural disasters, outbreaks of disease, or the effects of poverty. The Church teaches that everyone has a right to experience healing in heart, mind, and body.

The Sacrament of Anointing of the Sick continues Jesus' healing ministry.

The Sacrament of Anointing of the Sick celebrates Jesus' healing work in a special way. Those who receive the grace of this sacrament receive healing, strength, peace, and courage to face the difficulties that come from serious illness and from the challenges of old age. A person can receive the Sacrament of Anointing of the Sick as many times as needed.

From the time of the Apostles, the faithful have turned to the Church for healing and comfort. In the following biblical account from the letter of Saint James, we see the beginning of the Sacrament of Anointing of the Sick.

"Is anyone among you suffering? He should pray. Is anyone in good spirits? He should sing praise. Is anyone among you sick? He should summon the presbyters of the church, and they should pray over him and anoint [him] with oil in the name of the Lord, and the prayer of faith will save the sick person, and the Lord will raise him up. If he has committed any sins, he will be forgiven" (James 5:13–15).

Jesus' Passion and Death on the Cross give new meaning to suffering. Through our suffering, we can be united with Christ and his redemptive Passion.

The grace of the Sacrament of Anointing of the Sick

- renews our trust and faith in God
- unites us to Christ and to his suffering
- gives us the strength, peace, and courage we need to endure our suffering
- prepares us, when necessary, for death and the hope of eternal life with God
- restores us to health if that is God's will for us.

Activity

Anointing of the Sick celebrates Christ's healing work. Explain to a partner how the sacrament can help people even if they do not recover physically from their illness.

Partners in Faith

Saint Gianna Beretta Molla

Saint Gianna Beretta Molla was a doctor in Italy. As a doctor, she tried to save lives and respect the dignity of each person. When she was pregnant with her fourth child, she became ill. She decided to try to save her child's life, even if she died. Her baby was born, but a week later Gianna died. Her husband and her children attended her canonization ceremony in 2004.

Learn more about the life of Saint Gianna Beretta Molla.

Faith Words

Sacraments of Healing   **conversion**

 Show What You Know

State whether each statement is true or false by circling the correct answer.
Correct any false statements.

1. Anointing of the Sick renews our trust and faith in God.

(True) | False

_____

_____

2. The Sacraments of Healing include Baptism and Confirmation.

True | (False)

Penanß and reconsiliation

_____

3. Conversion is the work of the Church within us.

True | False

_____

_____

Live Your Faith

How can we experience conversion?

_____

_____

_____

_____

_____

How have you felt after receiving the Sacrament of Penance and Reconciliation?

_____

_____

_____

_____

_____

_____

Mini-Task

When someone is sick or going through a tough time, there is often nothing we can do to "fix it." Sometimes the best gift we can give another person is our presence. Indeed, visiting the sick is one way we can share God's loving presence.

Think of a time when someone was present to you as you were struggling with an illness or another challenge. How did his or her presence affect the way you felt?

Write a short story about someone who was present to another person in need. How did this comfort the person?

_____

_____

_____

_____

_____

_____

_____

_____

_____

_____

_____

_____

 Want to do more? Go to your Portfolio to continue this activity.

 At Home

Think of how the members of your family feel when they have been carrying around a heavy bag all day, and what a relief it is to put it down. What is the heaviest burden on your family's hearts right now? Together, tell God about that burden and tell him your family is ready to stop carrying it.

How are we strengthened for service to God and others?

All of the baptized are called to serve the Church through the common priesthood of the faithful. The Sacraments at the Service of Communion—Holy Orders and Matrimony—give men and women the special grace and strength to serve God and the Church through a particular vocation to which God has called them.

Go to the digital portal for a prayer of meditation.

"Holy Orders and Matrimony are directed towards the salvation of others; if they contribute as well to personal salvation, it is through service to others that they do so. They confer a particular mission in the Church and serve to build up the People of God."

Catechism of the Catholic Church, 1534

We are all called to serve the Church through the common priesthood of the faithful.

Faith Word

vocation see p. 259

We all share in Christ's priestly mission. All baptized Christians share in the common priesthood of the faithful, and we all share a common **vocation**, too. This vocation is to grow in holiness, share the message of Jesus' life and saving work, and serve one another and the Church. God calls each of us to live out our common vocation in a particular way. We do this as laypeople, consecrated religious, or ordained ministers.

In the Sacrament of Holy Orders, baptized men can be ordained as bishops, priests, and deacons. Through ordination, a baptized man becomes a representative of Jesus Christ, Head of the Church, as priest, prophet, and king. All three ordained ministries—bishops, priests, and deacons—are essential for the Church to exist and to function. Through these ministries, Jesus Christ builds up and leads his Church.

In the Old Covenant, priests were appointed to offer gifts and sacrifices for sins. This priesthood of the Old Covenant prefigures, or foretells, the ordained ministry of the New Covenant established through Jesus' sacrifice on the Cross. The Prayer of Consecration offered when a man is ordained as a bishop reminds us of the priesthood of the Old Covenant.

What do I know about our common vocation?

"God the Father of our Lord Jesus Christ, . . .
by your gracious word
you have established the plan of your Church.
From the beginning,
you chose the descendants of Abraham to be your holy nation.
You established rulers and priests,
and did not leave your sanctuary without ministers
to serve you."

Roman Pontifical, Prayer of Consecration, Ordination of Bishops, quoted in CCC ,1541

Did You Know?

Priests represent Christ in many different ways.

Men who are ordained in the Sacrament of Holy Orders serve the Church by teaching, leading divine worship, and governing the Church.

Jesus entrusted the Apostles with his own mission—to bring the Good News of salvation to the ends of the earth. Jesus sent out the Apostles to teach people and to baptize them. The Holy Spirit strengthened the Apostles to carry out this mission.

Everywhere they went, the Apostles gathered believers into local Church communities. They chose leaders and ministers for the community. The Apostles laid hands on the people they had chosen, and also commissioned them. Some of these leaders acted on behalf of the Apostles by preaching the Good News of Jesus Christ and sharing the Apostles' teachings. They continued the Apostles' ministry and were their successors. They were known as overseers because of their role in governing the local church. The word *bishop* comes from the Greek word for overseer.

Saint Paul preaching in Athens by Raphael, 1515.

The local leaders who worked with the bishops became known as priests. Those who assisted in the worship and service of the community were called deacons. As the Church continued to grow, the bishops, the successors of the Apostles, ordained others to continue the ministry of the Apostles. In this way, the leadership of the Church throughout history can be traced all the way back to the Apostles.

One Church, Many Cultures

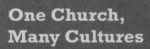

We are a worldwide Church, and our global view includes the work of Church leaders. Bishops from around the world attend regular meetings with the pope at the Vatican. They discuss issues that are important to the people and cultures of the different areas where the bishops minister. During these papal meetings, the pope speaks to bishops from each region about specific issues and then listens to their reports and concerns. From the pope and other Church officials to our local priests, deacons, and parishioners, we can all learn from one another.

Activity

In the Sacrament of Holy Orders, baptized men receive the grace of the Holy Spirit necessary to act in the name of Christ. List some things that bishops, priests, and deacons do to serve the Church.

_____

_____

_____

_____

_____

_____

_____

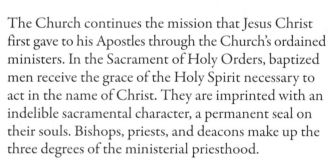

Faith Words

bishops see p. 257

priests see p. 258

deacons see p. 257

The Church continues the mission that Jesus Christ first gave to his Apostles through the Church's ordained ministers. In the Sacrament of Holy Orders, baptized men receive the grace of the Holy Spirit necessary to act in the name of Christ. They are imprinted with an indelible sacramental character, a permanent seal on their souls. Bishops, priests, and deacons make up the three degrees of the ministerial priesthood.

• The **bishops** are the successors of the Apostles. They carry out the mission, as given to the Apostles by Christ, of teaching, governing, and sanctifying the Church. Each diocese—the Catholic population in a geographical region—is headed by a bishop. Only bishops receive the fullness of the Sacrament of Holy Orders.

• **Priests** are ordained by a bishop and serve the Church by preaching and, most especially, by celebrating the Eucharist and other sacraments. Priests are co-workers with bishops.

• **Deacons** are ordained by a bishop to serve the Church in worship, governance, and charity. Although deacons cannot preside at the Eucharist, they have an important role in preaching and in works of charity. A deacon's ministry is always carried out under a bishop's authority.

What Makes Us Catholic?

In addition to Holy Orders and Matrimony, another vocation that is important in the life of the Church is consecrated religious life. Consecrated religious are men and women who make vows, or promises, of poverty, chastity, and obedience. These vows are called the evangelical counsels. They allow those in consecrated religious life to dedicate their lives to service and prayer. Consecrated religious sisters and brothers receive special gifts or graces of the Holy Spirit, called charisms, to help them live out their vocation. These charisms are often connected to the ministry of the founder of each religious community.

The Sacrament of Matrimony joins a man and a woman in a lifelong covenant of love with each other and God.

The **marriage covenant** is based in Christ's love for his Church. A baptized man and a baptized woman enter into a marriage covenant by exchanging vows. In these vows, they freely promise three things:

• to love each other for the rest of their lives

• to be faithful to each other—giving themselves only to each other—for the rest of their lives

• to accept children from God, and to raise those children in the Catholic faith.

Through the Sacrament of Matrimony, the man and woman receive the grace to live out these vows.

God founded marriage, and Christ made marriage a sacrament. The grace of the Sacrament of Matrimony helps the spouses love each other with the same love with which Christ has loved the Church, perfects their love, makes them more closely united, and sanctifies them (makes them holy).

Through their married love, the couple witnesses to God's love and faithfulness. They tell the world about God in a way that they could not do each on their own.

The Vatican II document *Gaudium et Spes* calls children "the supreme gift of marriage" (*GS* 50). When God blesses a married couple with children, the children contribute greatly to the good of their parents. Married couples share the fruits of their love for God and for each other with their children.

Faith Word

marriage covenant
see p. 258

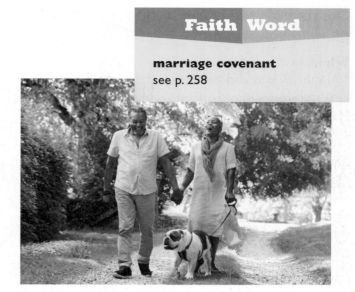

Parents also teach their children about Jesus Christ and the Catholic faith.

Christ and the Church teach us that the marriage covenant cannot be broken except by death. The sacramental marriage covenant is lifelong. If one spouse dies, the other is free to remarry. Catholics who are divorced and remarried cannot receive the Eucharist unless their first marriage has been annulled by the Church. (An annulment is the Church's declaration that a marriage is "null," meaning that the woman and man were not able to be sacramentally married to begin with.) Nevertheless, they can still lead Christian lives, attend Mass, and raise their children as Catholics.

Partners in Faith

Saint John XXIII

Saint John XXIII was 76 years old when he was elected pope in 1958. He surprised everyone when, not long after his election, he announced the Second Vatican Council. He wanted the Church to place more emphasis on evangelization and to be more open to certain aspects of modern culture. He was a strong supporter of human rights and the equality of all people and was known as "Good Pope John."

 Learn more about the life of Saint John XXIII.

Our families are called to be the light of Christ in the world.

Who first taught you about Jesus Christ and his Church? Where did you first learn to pray and first hear the stories of our ancestors in faith? If you are like most people, you probably first learned about the Church, the "family of God," in your own family.

Jesus was born into and grew up in a family, too—the Holy Family of Joseph and Mary. We can imagine Jesus, as a young boy, praying, celebrating, hearing the Scriptures, and participating in the rituals and traditions of the Jewish faith.

In the early Church, the seeds of faith were sown in households where families celebrated the Eucharist and lived the Gospel message. The *Catechism of the Catholic Church* explains that "These families who became believers were islands of Christian life in an unbelieving world" (*CCC*, 1655).

Just as the first Christian families were communities of faith, hope, and love, today's Christian families are also called to be the Light of Christ in the world. Every family is called to be a **domestic church**, or a "church in the home." How does this happen?

Faith Word

domestic church see p. 257

In his Apostolic Exhortation *On the Family*, Pope John Paul II said the Catholic family should "become more and more what it is, . . . a community of life and love." Families reflect the light of Christ in the world when they share the Catholic faith, celebrate rituals, pray together, deepen their own relationships, and reach out to those in need. Families also reflect the light of Christ when they forgive one another and when they follow the Ten Commandments, the Beatitudes, and Christ's example.

God is present in all the joys, the sorrows, the ordinary and extraordinary moments, and even the messiness of family life. Family is where we first learn that God is always with us, and where we first learn what it means to be a disciple of Jesus. The love of Christ is at the heart of every Christian family. That love is meant to shine out into the world for all to see.

Activity

Write a blessing for your family. Be sure to include the names of each person. Once you have written your blessing, sit for a few minutes and pray your blessing prayer. Exchange your prayer with a partner and pray for his or her family as well.

Faith Words			
vocation	**bishops**	**priests**	**deacons**
marriage covenant		**domestic church**	

 ## Show What You Know

Draw a line to match each term to its definition.

1. priests

2. domestic church

3. deacons

4. marriage covenant

5. bishops

6. vocation

the church of the home, which every Christian family is called to be

a baptized man and a baptized woman exchange vows of fidelity, love, and an openness to life and to the raising of children in the Catholic faith

ordained ministers who serve the Church by preaching and most especially by celebrating the Eucharist and other sacraments

baptized men who are ordained to serve the Church in worship, governance, and charity

the successors of the Apostles who are ordained to continue the Apostles' mission of teaching, governing, and sanctifying the Church

God's call to each person to serve him in a special way

Live Your Faith

How you do think it would feel to be called to ordained ministry?

_____

_____

_____

_____

_____

_____

What rituals in your family help you remember your role as part of the Church?

_____

_____

_____

_____

_____

_____

How do I share in the mission of Jesus Christ?

Mini-Task

We pray to thank God for the many gifts in our lives and to ask for blessings for the days ahead. As a family, you may pray together most often at mealtimes.

Ask if you can pray in a new way at mealtime. After saying grace, go around the table, giving time for all family members to say how they will share in the mission of Jesus Christ.

In the space below, write down three ways that you will share in the mission of Jesus Christ.

Family Prayer Prompt

I will share in the mission of Jesus Christ by . . .

_____

_____

_____

_____

_____

_____

_____

_____

_____

 Want to do more? Go to your Portfolio to continue this activity.

God calls all families to be a light to the world. Talk with your family members about ways your family can be a light to the world. Suggested ways to shine a light can be praying for those in need, sharing God's joy with other families, and serving families who need food and clothing.

Unit 3
The Faith Lived

Preaching in the Synagogue

Unit Prayer

Leader: Saint Dominic believed that he was not capable of doing "big things." But Jesus taught us that we all can do great things by simply living our faith, as Saint Dominic realized. Let us listen to stories of people among us who have done great things by simply living their faith.

Listen to stories of missionary disciples among us.

Leader: Jesus, you taught us to find you in the outcasts of this world. Help us to be your eyes and hands in the world.

All: We are your eyes and hands in the world.

Leader: Jesus, you reached out to people who were sick or poor. Help us to be your eyes and hands in the world.

All: We are your eyes and hands in the world.

Leader: Jesus, you taught us to live as children of God.

All: We are your eyes and hands in the world.

Leader: Jesus, you showed us how to live a life of love.

All: We are your eyes and hands in the world.

(*End the Unit Prayer by singing the song for this unit.*)

Unit Song: "I Send You Out," John Angotti

Missionary Discipleship

Have you ever reached out to someone who was an "outcast"—lonely, sad, or afraid? What did you do? How do you think that person felt? How did you feel?

How do we know God loves us?

Every human, with the dignity of being created in God's image, is sacred. God created us with free will that allows us to make choices and accept their consequences. God's natural law is written on our hearts and is part of our human reason. It guides us in knowing right from wrong and in choosing what is good and true. It is the foundation for all just rules and laws in human society. However, because of the effects of Original Sin, we are not always able to use our reason and to follow God's law. Fortunately, all who believe in Christ have a new life in the Holy Spirit, a life that will reach its fulfillment in the glory of heaven.

Go to the digital portal for a prayer of praise.

"God created mankind in his image;
in the image of God he created them;
male and female he created them."

Genesis 1:27

God created us in his image to share in his life and love forever.

God created *all* people in his image. Not just you, and not just your family and friends, but *every single* person. God reveals himself through us. God's desire for every person is to share in eternal happiness with him.

God also has a plan for each one of us. Even before we were born—in fact, for all eternity—God has been calling us to share in his life and love (see Jeremiah 1:4–5).

God has created each one of us with a **soul**, the spiritual dimension of our being that gives us life and that lives forever. Sacred Scripture refers to the human soul as God's breath within us that makes us human (see Genesis 2:7). Our physical bodies are animated or "made alive" by our spiritual souls.

God has also given us minds that can reason and think, dream and imagine. With our intellect, we can understand creation. Through reason, we can recognize the voice of God that urges us "to do what is good and avoid what is evil" (*Catechism of the Catholic Church*, 1706). In addition, because God has given us the gift of **free will**, we can freely choose to do right or wrong. When our reason and will are informed by

faith and strengthened by grace, we can choose to follow God's law: to love him and to love our neighbor as ourselves.

God's desire for all people is that we share in his life and love. Free will is the gift that, informed by our faith, allows us to freely respond to God's grace and choose the path of beatitude—life with God forever. By freely choosing to respond to God's grace, we have the freedom to choose what is good and holy. We have the freedom to choose to follow God.

Faith Words

soul see p. 259

free will see p. 257

Activity

Divide into two groups to talk about how these things are part of our soul:

intellect   will

Have each group choose one aspect of the soul to discuss. After your discussion, explain your thoughts to the rest of the group.

What difference does free will make in my life?

Did You Know?

Human dignity is the guiding principle of Catholic social teaching.

Human dignity means that every life is sacred.

By the creative action of God, human life came to be. God created humanity to be different from the rest of creation. God created us in his own image and likeness. This is the inherent dignity that God has given to every person. We are God's own! Life is in God's hands:

"Which of all these does not know
　　that the hand of God has done this?
In his hand is the soul of every living thing,
　　and the life breath of all mortal flesh."

(Job 12:9–10)

Every human life is sacred, from the moment of conception to natural death. Our society today grapples with the good or evil of many life issues. At the root of every one of the Church's teachings about these issues is this fundamental belief in the sacredness and dignity of the human person. God alone is the Lord of life.

"You formed my inmost being;
　　you knit me in my mother's womb.
I praise you, because I am wonderfully made;
　　wonderful are your works!
My very self you know."

(Psalm 139:13–14)

What Makes Us Catholic?

We know from Scripture that we are "wonderfully made" and that each of us reflects God. Jesus himself took on our human life in the Incarnation. The Incarnation reminds us of our innate human dignity, as we are made in the image and likeness of God. Being made in God's image and likeness is the basis of the Church's teaching that all life is sacred, from the moment of conception to natural death. When a woman is pregnant, the Church prays: "God, author of all life, / bless, we pray, this unborn child; / give constant protection" (*Rite for the Blessing of a Child in the Womb*).

Peaceful civil rights marches of twentieth-century America helped bring about laws protecting the human dignity of all people.

Free will is the basis of moral responsibility.

When was the last time you heard—or said to someone—"Don't do that!"? We often say this to warn people that what they are about to do is physically, emotionally, or spiritually harmful, or wrong. At that point, the person has a choice. The result of that choice will be that person's responsibility. In this situation, a person is exercising his or her freedom, the power we have "to act or not to act, to do this or that" (*CCC*, 1731).

God has given us the gift of his grace and the gift of free will. Together, these gifts shape our choices and actions. Our human dignity includes the responsibility of making decisions. Free will allows us to make choices and accept their consequences. No one has the right to stop us from using free will, or to force us to use it to choose something evil. Human freedom, when used for the glory of God, is a force for goodness and truth in the world.

Throughout salvation history, God has held his people accountable for their actions. After our first parents ate from the Tree of the Knowledge of Good and Evil, God said to them: "What is this you have done?" (Genesis 3:13). After Cain murdered his brother, Abel, God asked him: "What have you done? Your brother's blood cries out to me from the ground!" (Genesis 4:10). God told them that their actions were their responsibility, not someone else's.

The *Catechism* tells us that each of us has a right to "be recognized as a free and responsible being. All owe to each other this duty of respect. The *right to the exercise of freedom*, especially in moral and religious matters, is an inalienable requirement of the dignity of the human person" (*CCC*, 1738).

Freedom does not mean that we have a right to say or do anything and everything. Saying and doing whatever we want, whenever we want, implies that we are not in relationship with others. But, in fact, we are deeply connected with other human beings, and we are bound by the duty of respect and dignity that we owe to them.

When we do whatever we want without regard for others, we sin against God, self, and neighbor. These sins imprison us and make us less free. Human freedom is freedom to do what we ought, not what we want.

The natural law leads us to seek what is good.

Over the course of salvation history, God's **natural law** has been planted in the heart of every person. It is a rational awareness, a voice of reason, and a moral sense within us. Natural law moves us to seek God and choose what is good and true. Every human being has the capacity, through our use of reason, to identify what is good and what is evil. These common principles can unite us and form the foundation for civil rules and laws.

Faith Word

natural law see p. 258

In the Old Testament account of Cain and Abel, Cain killed his brother Abel (see Genesis 4:1–16). God asked Cain: "What have you done?" Cain knew what he had done and that it was wrong. Even though God had not yet given his people the Fifth Commandment ("you shall not kill"), God had planted the knowledge of what is good and true—his natural law—on Cain's heart.

Activity

Review the Ten Commandments. Choose two or three and consider how each is reasonable. For example, why is it reasonable to honor our parents and respect those who have authority over us? Is it ever reasonable or morally acceptable to disobey people in positions of authority? Discuss with the larger group.

In the Old Testament, God's people were having difficulty following the law that God had planted on their hearts. So God gave his people the Ten Commandments to make his ways known to them. The commandments reminded the people of the laws that God had written on their hearts (see Exodus 20:1–17). The commandments laid the foundation for how the people were to live in a way that reflects God's image. The commandments set down actions that are contrary to the love of God and neighbor (what *not* to do) and actions that are essential for loving God and neighbor (what *to* do).

In the New Testament, Jesus Christ told his disciples to follow the commandments and said that he had come to fulfill them (see Matthew 5:17). Jesus' New Law, the law of love, which he taught in the Sermon on the Mount (see Matthew 5–7), revealed the deeper, hidden meaning of the Old Law. Jesus' law invites all people to follow a new commandment: "Love one another as I love you" (John 15:12).

One Church, Many Cultures

The law of God within us—natural law—is our compass to guide us toward a good and moral life. We see the influence of natural law in cultures around the world. We also see societies that do not have civil laws that honor human dignity. The Church works hard to protect human rights around the globe, sometimes under difficult or dangerous circumstances. This includes working to stop prejudice, violence, slavery, and other unjust situations. The Church helps us to see one another as children of God.

Saint Thomas Aquinas' writings are known for helping us to understand the Bible and Church teachings. He described God's natural law as "nothing other than the light of understanding placed in us by God; through it we know what we must do and what we must avoid. God has given this light or law at the creation" (see *CCC*, 1955).

Notice what Saint Thomas Aquinas did not say about the natural law. He *did not* say that this light or law is reserved for a select few. Instead, God has given this light or law to *everyone*. God's natural law binds us together as one human family.

However, Original Sin makes following the natural law difficult. Because of the Fall, we all have a tendency to make decisions based on our feelings and self-interests rather than on reason. This can make it hard for us to see clearly what is right and what is wrong.

God's natural law remains permanent, as it has been throughout history. It is the foundation for all just human rules and civil laws; it is enduring and will never change.

Partners in Faith

Saint Joan of France

Saint Joan of France lived with disabilities. She was never fully healthy, and she walked with a limp. At age 12, she was married to the Duke of Orleans, who mistreated her. Eventually their marriage was annulled by the Church because Joan and the duke had not been able to freely consent to the marriage. Saint Joan then founded a religious order of nuns. Joan never let her disabilities get in the way of her service to God.

 Learn more about the life of Saint Joan of France.

Faith Words

soul   free will   natural law

 Show What You Know

Explain each term in your own words.

1. free will

_____
_____
_____
_____

2. natural law

_____
_____
_____

3. soul

_____
_____
_____
_____
_____

Live Your Faith

God gave the natural law to everyone. In what ways can you follow natural law
the next time you are tempted to do something you know is wrong?

_____
_____
_____
_____

In what ways do your heart, mind, body, and soul work together to help you
live as Christ's disciple?

_____
_____
_____
_____

Lesson 11
Portfolio

How do I show God's love to others?

Mini-Task

We know that every person has inborn dignity because every person was created in the image and likeness of God. Human dignity is the foundation of Catholic social teaching.

Talk about these questions with your group:

Who are the people or groups in our society who are often not shown dignity or respect? For example:

- elderly people
- people who suffer from mental illness
- people with disabilities
- unborn children
- people from different countries or races

What other examples can you think of?

How do we show dignity or respect? How can you use your words and actions to help others feel valued?

In the space, create a sign you might hold up at a rally to show support for a group or individual who is not being treated with dignity and respect.

 Want to do more? Go to your Portfolio to continue this activity.

With your family, discuss the rules that your family follows. How are these rules rooted in natural law?

How do we respond to God's love?

God promised to love his people, always. God's covenant was fulfilled in Jesus, who revealed its true meaning. Jesus gave us the Beatitudes. They express the kind of life we are called to live in order to share in eternal happiness. God's Word guides our conscience to make choices that are good and true. The virtues and the gifts of the Holy Spirit guide us to relationship with the Blessed Trinity. We are called to work for justice and solidarity to bring about God's Kingdom.

 Go to the digital portal for a prayer of thanksgiving.

"For this reason he is mediator of a new covenant: since a death has taken place for deliverance from transgressions under the first covenant, those who are called may receive the promised eternal inheritance."

Hebrews 9:15

God's law leads us to eternal happiness with him.

Jesus Christ is the fullness of Divine Revelation. This means that God has revealed everything we need to know for our salvation in the life of Jesus. Jesus is the mediator of the New Covenant who came to fulfill the Old Covenant, or Old Law.

We first learn of God's covenant promises to his Chosen People in the stories of the patriarchs in the Old Testament. God then gave his people the Law to guide them in choosing goodness and truth. God's Law, which he proclaimed through Moses (see Exodus 20:1–17), set forth the requirements for living in a right relationship with God.

The books of the Old Testament that appear in the Pentateuch present various aspects of God's Law. These books are also known as the Torah. They are Genesis, Exodus, Leviticus, Numbers, and Deuteronomy. God gradually revealed, during the times of the kings and prophets, what it meant to be in a covenant relationship with him. Wisdom literature, found in the books of Proverbs, Sirach, and Wisdom, set forth practical advice for how to live a virtuous life.

In Jesus, the Old Covenant is fulfilled. Jesus' Paschal Mystery—his life, Death, Resurrection, and Ascension—fulfills the Old Covenant. Jesus is the "light for the nations" prophesied in the Book of Isaiah.

> *"I formed you, and set you as a covenant for the people, a light for the nations."*
>
> Isaiah 42:6

How do I share in God's grace?

Jesus, the Son of God, fulfilled the Old Law by revealing its true meaning in his own Person (in his teachings, actions, and witness). In a definitive way, Jesus established and demonstrated the New Law—which is a law of grace, love, and mercy—through the new and everlasting covenant. Jesus affirmed this covenant with his disciples at the Last Supper, and he confirmed it through his suffering, Death, and Resurrection. In the Sermon on the Mount (see Matthew 5–7), Jesus gave us the Beatitudes (see Matthew 5:3–12), which express the kind of life every Christian is called to live. They are the actions and attitudes of Christ that lead toward eternal happiness and blessedness. The Beatitudes point us toward the Kingdom of Heaven.

Activity

With a partner, choose one of the Beatitudes (see page 248 in your book). Write that Beatitude in modern-day words, and turn to and talk with another pair of students. Try to guess each other's modern Beatitudes.

Did You Know?

We are a covenant people.

The Word of God helps to inform our conscience and guide our moral choices.

Every human being has a **conscience**. A well-formed conscience leads us to use our reason to know the difference between good and evil, right and wrong. This conscience is like an inner voice. In the sanctuary of our conscience, we are "alone with God whose voice echoes in [our] depths" (*CCC*, 1776). Our conscience is that nudge, or push, we experience from within that directs us to do good and to avoid evil. This nudge comes from God. When we listen to our conscience, we can hear God speaking, and we must always obey.

Our conscience must be carefully formed in what is good and true so that the choices we make correspond with God's plan for us. Educating our conscience is a lifelong task. The Word of God plays a central role in the formation of our conscience. In faith and in prayer, we must make Sacred Scripture part of our lives and always try to put it into practice. The writer of the Book of Psalms described formation of conscience this way:

"I have more understanding than my elders,
　　because I keep your precepts.
I keep my steps from every evil path,
　　that I may observe your word.
From your judgments I do not turn,
　　for you have instructed me.
How sweet to my tongue is your promise,
　　sweeter than honey to my mouth!
Through your precepts I gain understanding;
　　therefore I hate all false ways.
Your word is a lamp for my feet,
　　a light for my path"　(Psalm 119:100–105).

God's Word lights our path in the way of truth and goodness.

Faith Word

conscience see p. 257

Activity

Reread Psalm 119:100–105. Now write the psalm in modern language with modern imagery. Once you have rewritten the psalm, choose a partner and create a new piece, alternating lines. Read your new psalm to your group.

One Church, Many Cultures

Light is a powerful image in our Church. The Cathedral of Christ the Light in Oakland, California, is a place of beauty, community, and celebration. Its members are from many different backgrounds, including Vietnamese, Filipino, and Latin American. They participate in cultural festivals and events as well as regular Masses and other Church celebrations. Dedicated to Christ as "the Light of the World" and "light of all nations," the cathedral was built to resemble an ark, welcoming and giving safety to all. Light streams through the many windows of the cathedral, including a fifty-eight-foot-tall window that shows Christ as King.

The virtues and the gifts of the Holy Spirit guide us to a healthy relationship with the Trinity.

Faith Word

Theological Virtues
see p. 259

What do you think would be the characteristics of the perfect human community? Perhaps the Theological and Cardinal Virtues and the gifts of the Holy Spirit would be on your list. These virtues and gifts guide us to live in right relationship with the Blessed Trinity and with one another. To find the most perfect communion, we have to look no further than the Blessed Trinity. The Trinity is a communion of Persons—God the Father, God the Son, and God the Holy Spirit. This means that each Person is completely God—not part of God or partially God. Yet, at the same time, there is only One God. This mystery is very difficult to explain in words! Yet it is the central mystery of the Christian faith and of Christian life. We could never know this mystery on our own, so, in great love, God has revealed it to us. And our vocation as the human community is to show forth the image of God, the Blessed Trinity. Let's take a closer look at how the Theological and Cardinal Virtues and the gifts of the Holy Spirit guide us to this end.

The **Theological Virtues** of faith, hope, and love have their origin in God. They are gifts from God that help us to live in relationship with the Blessed Trinity. They bring us closer to God and increase our desire to be with him forever. They are the reasons it is possible for us to have a relationship with God—the Father, the Son, and the Holy Spirit.

- *Faith* enables us to believe in God and all that the Church teaches us.

- *Hope* enables us to trust in God's promise that we will share in his life forever.

- *Love* enables us to love our neighbor out of our love for God (see *CCC*, 1822).

"So faith, hope, love remain, these three; but the greatest of these is love."

1 Corinthians 13:13

Faith Word

Cardinal Virtues see p. 257

United Nations peacekeepers on a training mission in Bangladesh

The gifts of the Holy Spirit also support the moral life of Christians by helping us to live in right relationship with the Blessed Trinity and with one another. These seven gifts are wisdom, understanding, counsel, fortitude, knowledge, piety, and fear of the Lord. These gifts perfect the virtues. They also make us open to divine inspiration so that we are ready and willing to do all that God asks of us.

"The spirit of the Lord shall rest upon him:
   a spirit of wisdom and of understanding,
A spirit of counsel and of strength,
   a spirit of knowledge and of fear of the Lord,
   and his delight shall be the fear of the Lord."

(Isaiah 11:2–3)

The **Cardinal Virtues**—also called the moral virtues—of prudence, justice, temperance, and fortitude are what the *Catechism* calls the "fruit and seed of morally good acts" (*CCC*, 1804). This means that these virtues should guide our actions, emotions, and choices in accordance with reason and faith. We can grow as virtuous people through education and by making good decisions, even when it is difficult. All the other human virtues are grouped around the four Cardinal Virtues.

- *Prudence* enables us to call on reason to determine the true good in every situation.
- *Justice* enables us to give God and neighbor their due.
- *Temperance* enables us to manage our desires and to achieve a healthy, balanced attitude toward material possessions.
- *Fortitude* enables us to use strength or courage to make sound decisions, especially in the face of difficulties or challenges.

"Or if one loves righteousness,
   whose works are virtues,

She teaches moderation and prudence,
   righteousness and fortitude,
   and nothing in life is more useful than these."

(Wisdom 8:7)

What Makes Us Catholic?

We can practice the Cardinal Virtues in different life situations. When we do this, we show others what it means to be a follower of Christ. Prudence gives us the ability to stay calm and find peaceful solutions to problems. Justice inspires us to stand up for human rights around the world. Temperance helps us show that people are more important than possessions or rewards. Fortitude allows us to speak and act on what we believe on behalf of ourselves and other people. As Catholics, we can act as models of virtue in our communities.

Faith Words

common good see p. 257

justice see p. 258

solidarity see p. 259

We are called to work for the common good.

God calls every person to the same end: to communion with him. The human community is called by God to be rooted in his truth, love, and unity. The Church plays a special role in helping people to encounter God and follow his will.

We all live in community and have a fundamental need to be in relationships with other people. Through these relationships, we develop our full potential and respond to God's call to life in communion with him. Because we are part of one human family—united with all people, both living and deceased—we are called to participate in and contribute to the life of society.

Our call to participate in society begins in the most basic unit of society, the family. We learn and grow in the ways of God within our families. In a homily, Pope Francis once said that "Sorry," "Excuse me," and "Thank you" are "essential words for our life in common" as a family (October 13, 2013, Holy Mass for the Marian Day on the occasion of the Year of Faith).

But we don't remain behind closed doors, interacting only with our own families. Rather, we take into the world what we learn in our families, the virtues we practice, and the life-giving ways of relating to one another. All of these good habits and practices that we have learned in our families can help us to make a positive contribution to the wider community, the larger family of God.

In our families, we first begin to understand that our own good is directly related to the common good. The **common good** concerns the life of all people. It means working to establish social and economic conditions that allow people, either as groups or as individuals, to live with dignity and develop themselves and the society in which we live.

Working for the common good of society and all people requires a commitment to justice and solidarity. We work toward **justice** when God and others are given their due. We work toward **solidarity** when our actions reflect a love for all people, regardless of racial, religious, economic, or cultural differences. We respect the needs of others and work toward the common good.

Partners in Faith

Saint Jerome

Saint Jerome is best known for having translated the Bible into Latin. His translation is known as the *Vulgate*. He wrote many commentaries on the Gospels. He also studied classical literature, but after a serious illness, he devoted himself exclusively to Scripture. As proof that saints are not always the sweetest people, Jerome was also known for being slightly cranky—one reason he may have lived alone in the desert.

 Learn more about the life of Saint Jerome.

Faith Words

conscience   **Theological Virtues**

Cardinal Virtues   **common good**

justice   **solidarity**

 Show What You Know

Draw a line to match each term to its definition.

1. Theological Virtues

2. justice

3. solidarity

4. Cardinal Virtues

5. conscience

the moral virtue that consists in giving God and neighbor their due

faith, hope, and love

the Christian virtue that involves a love for all people and respects the needs of others

the ability to use reason to know the difference between good and evil

prudence, justice, fortitude, and temperance

Live Your Faith

In what way does the virtue of hope help you in your faith journey?

_____

_____

_____

_____

_____

_____

_____

In what ways do you promote the common good in your life?

_____

_____

_____

_____

_____

_____

_____

_____

How do I respond to God's love?

Mini-Task

Cardinal Virtues are ways we respond to God's love and live a Christian moral life.
Choose one virtue that you would like to explore. In what ways will you practice this virtue?

Prudence

_____

_____

_____

Justice

_____

_____

_____

Fortitude

_____

_____

_____

Temperance

_____

_____

_____

Create a photo essay depicting what it means to live out your chosen virtue.

Want to do more? Go to your Portfolio to continue this activity.

At Home

What virtues do you think are the strongest in your family's life? The weakest?
Pray this week for strength in the areas where you know God is calling your family
to grow stronger.

How does God teach us to love?

The Ten Commandments are a foundation for how to live faithfully with love for God and neighbor. They remind us that our relationship with God is our primary concern. They give us a model for loving others and living in God's truth. The laws of God and the Church guide our moral choices and help us build a society of truth, justice, and solidarity.

Go to the digital portal for a meditation prayer.

"You shall love the Lord, your God, with all your heart, with all your soul, and with all your mind. This is the greatest and the first commandment. The second is like it: You shall love your neighbor as yourself. The whole law and the prophets depend on these two commandments."

Matthew 22:37–40

God's laws help us stay faithful to him and his covenant.

Most of us have found ourselves in situations in which we know the right thing to do, but we struggle to do it. This has been the story of God's people throughout salvation history. God and Abraham entered into a covenant: God would be faithful to his people and God's people would be faithful to him.

God's Chosen People struggled to live in right relationship with him. While on their way to the Promised Land, they were hungry, thirsty, and tired. So they grumbled, complained, and were angry at Moses. Yet God, ever faithful, provided for their physical needs. God gave them manna (a kind of bread) to eat (see Exodus 16) and water from the rock to drink (see Exodus 17). God also provided for their spiritual needs by giving them the **Ten Commandments**, the Old Law. These commandments would help the Israelites hold up their side of the covenant and remain faithful to God. The Old Law would prepare God's people for the New Covenant that Jesus would begin.

The Ten Commandments help us to understand how to live as the People of God. They make God's call and ways known to us. They tell us how to live without offending God or harming other people and ourselves.

Faith Word

Ten Commandments
see p. 259

 Ten Commandments

When have I struggled to do the right thing?

Did You Know?

 Laws help to define us.

The Ten Commandments establish that God is our first priority.

Do you like using lists? Maybe you know people who use lists to stay on top of what needs to get done. Some of these people are so organized, they prioritize what is on their lists by identifying what is most important or what needs to be done first.

Love of God needs to be at the top of our lists. Our relationship with God is at the very center, the heart, of our lives. Everything about our lives revolves around, comes from, points to, and depends on God's presence. The first three commandments establish this truth. They tell us to love, worship, and serve only God, to keep the Lord God's name holy, and to keep the Lord God's day holy. What do these three commandments have in common? The name *God*.

Think about names for a moment. When you tell your name to others, you're sharing a part of yourself, for your name represents you. And you're trusting that others are not going to abuse your name, make fun of your name, or call you names. You trust that they are going to respect you and your name, that your name will not become associated with words of hatred, gossip, or disrespect. The *Catechism of the Catholic Church* states: "The gift of a name belongs to the order of trust and intimacy" (*CCC*, 2143).

In Jewish biblical tradition, a name represented the nature and essence of the person named. It represented that person's reputation. And the name was treated with the same respect as the person it represented. It follows, then, that the name *God* was more than a title of honor. The name *God* represented the divine nature and the proper relationship between him and his people. The writers of the Old Testament often spoke of the name of God as being equal to the divine presence. Honoring the name of God meant being faithful to God's covenant. It especially meant following the first three commandments, all focused on love of, and respect for, the one, true God.

God revealed his name to those who believed in him. And we can see why the very name of God is holy. God's name belongs at the top of our list. God is our first priority.

Activity

Write a paragraph about your day. What do you think is the most important thing you did? How important was spending time with God? If someone else read your paragraph, what would they decide was the most important thing you did?

What Makes Us Catholic?

According to Jewish tradition, an individual's name represents the very nature and essence of the person. Names are important in the Catholic faith, too. Before celebrating the Sacrament of Confirmation, candidates choose a Confirmation name. This may be their baptismal name—the name by which they became children of God. Or they may choose the name of a saint. The saint may be someone who has inspired their journey in the Catholic faith. Or the chosen saint may be associated with a particular devotion, gift, or faith community that interests the candidate.

The Ten Commandments guide our actions toward others.

The Ten Commandments are the laws of the Old Covenant. If God's people lived by the Ten Commandments, they kept their covenant relationship with God. He was their God, and they were his people. We can find the commandments in Exodus chapter 20. God also gave Moses other laws to help the people, and these are recorded in the Book of Leviticus.

Growing up in a Jewish family, Jesus was taught the Ten Commandments. He lived by God's laws. As disciples of Jesus, we also follow the Ten Commandments. They are a foundation for living the New Covenant that God enters into with us at Baptism. They provide a model for loving others and living in God's truth.

In the Old Testament, Moses gave the people all the laws that God had given him. The Israelites, God's People, agreed to follow these laws. Moses then set up a stone altar with twelve pillars. The pillars represented the twelve tribes of Israel, the descendants of the twelve sons of Jacob. Moses then sealed the covenant by sacrificing some young bulls as a peace offering to God. Moses sprinkled some of the blood from the bulls, saying: "This is the blood of the covenant which the LORD has made with you according to all these words" (Exodus 24:8).

According to Christian interpretation, the twelve pillars of the stone altar also symbolize the twelve Apostles, the men with whom Jesus shared his ministry in a special way. Jesus Christ would send them out to spread the Good News that he was the Son of God, sent to save all people. Before his Death, Jesus celebrated the Passover meal with his Apostles. At this meal, which Christians call the Last Supper, Jesus said: "This cup is the new covenant in my blood, which will be shed for you" (Luke 22:20).

Last Supper of Christ by Leopold Kupelwieser, fresco, 1889

One Church, Many Cultures

God sealed a new covenant with his people through Christ's sacrifice on the Cross. In Ethiopia, Catholics have a special way of honoring this symbol of our salvation. Every September, they gather for a feast called *Meskel*. The celebration begins with the lighting of a large bonfire. It is believed that in the fourth century, the smoke of a fire led Saint Helena to the cross on which Christ suffered and died. The celebration of Meskel continues the following day when the people return to the site of the bonfire. They use the ashes to mark their foreheads with a Sign of the Cross.

Jesus Christ offered his own life to save us and to free us from sin. Jesus came to fulfill the Ten Commandments. So this *New* Covenant between God and his people has been sealed with Jesus' blood, not the blood of animals. Through this New Covenant, it is possible for us to share in God's life and love. We celebrate the New Covenant at each celebration of the Eucharist.

We look to the Ten Commandments, fulfilled in Jesus, as a model for how to love others and live in God's truth. Reflect on the ways the Fourth through Tenth Commandments guide you in loving others and living God's truth.

Fourth Commandment: Honor your father and your mother.

- In what ways do you show that you respect your parents and the rules they set for you?
- How do you honor others in positions of authority in your life, such as teachers and priests?

Fifth Commandment: You shall not kill.

- Do you have the courage to speak out against practices such as abortion and euthanasia, that violate a person's right to life?
- In what ways are you a peacemaker?

Sixth Commandment: You shall not commit adultery.

- How do you show respect for your own sexuality and that of others?
- How do you express friendship and love with others in appropriate ways?

Seventh Commandment: You shall not steal.

- How do you practice justice and charity?
- How do you treat other people's belongings?
- Do you keep your promises?

Eighth Commandment: You shall not bear false witness against your neighbor.

- Do you speak well of others?
- Do you tell the truth?

Ninth Commandment: You shall not covet your neighbor's wife.

- Is your heart focused on God?
- Do you respect the dignity of others?

Tenth Commandment: You shall not covet your neighbor's goods.

- Are you possessive of your own things?
- In what ways do you share your gifts with others?
- Are you jealous or envious of what other people possess?

Activity

List three ways the Ten Commandments help God's people live holy lives.

_____

_____

_____

List three ways the Eucharist helps us live holy lives.

_____

_____

_____

Compare your list with a partner's list. In what ways is the Eucharist like the Ten Commandments? In what ways is it different?

God's laws and the Church guide our moral choices.

We have learned how the laws of God and the Church guide our moral choices. These laws aren't meant to be tucked away and used only within our homes or churches. God's laws also guide how we behave as members of the broader community and society. They guide the choices we make in our towns and cities, and beyond.

As disciples of Jesus Christ, we have the duty and responsibility to work together with others to build up society in a spirit of truth, justice, solidarity, and freedom. We strive to reflect the light of Christ in society. We help to bring about the Kingdom of God by making morally good choices.

Sometimes secular or civil law contradicts moral law, or God's Law. In these instances, we must always obey God and follow a well-formed conscience. The Apostles faced this issue in the Acts of the Apostles when the high priest confronted them about teaching in Jesus' name:

"[T]he high priest questioned them, 'We gave you strict orders . . . to stop teaching in that name. Yet you have filled Jerusalem with your teaching and want to bring this man's blood upon us.' But Peter and the apostles said in reply, 'We must obey God rather than men. The God of our ancestors raised Jesus, though you had him killed by hanging him on a tree. God exalted him at his right hand as leader and savior to grant Israel repentance and forgiveness of sins. We are witnesses of these things, as is the holy Spirit that God has given to those who obey him.'"

(Acts of the Apostles 5:27–32)

Partners in Faith

Venerable Fulton Sheen

Venerable Fulton Sheen was one of the first people to use television as a means of spreading the Gospel. His show, *Life Is Worth Living*, earned him two Emmy awards. He also wrote seventy-three books. He understood that belief and action must be combined. If we know the commandments but we don't put God first, that knowledge will not make a difference in our lives. Venerable Sheen said: "If you do not worship God, you worship something, and nine times out of ten it will be yourself."

 Learn more about the life of Venerable Fulton Sheen.

Faith Word

Ten Commandments

Show What You Know

Complete the following sentences.

1. _____ is our first priority.

2. The Fourth through Tenth Commandments guide us in loving others and living God's _____.

3. God's laws and the Church guide our _____ choices.

4. The _____ provide a model for loving others and living in God's truth.

Live Your Faith

In what ways can the Ten Commandments help you when you need to make a hard choice?

_____

_____

_____

_____

_____

_____

_____

_____

In what ways do you keep God at the top of your list?

_____

_____

_____

_____

_____

_____

_____

_____

_____

How do God's laws lead me
to happiness?

Mini-Task

President Theodore Roosevelt said: "Comparison is the thief of joy." In our digital culture, it is easy to experience jealousy or envy when we compare ourselves with others who seem to have a "perfect" or better life. The Ninth and Tenth Commandments remind us that wanting what others have, or what they seem to have, goes against God's plan for us.

Plan a social media page to help young people fight envy with gratitude. Think of six things someone your age should be grateful for right now. Draw a picture of, or write about, each one below.

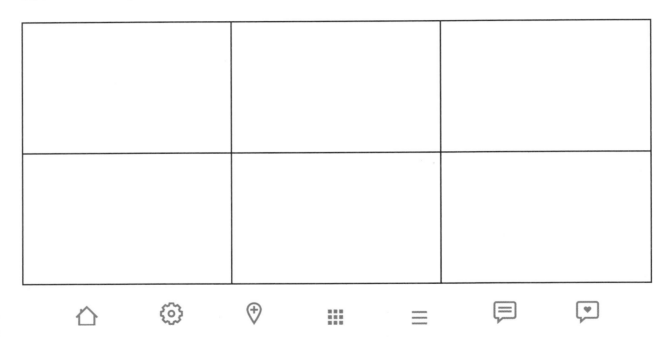

Want to do more? Go to your Portfolio to continue this activity.

At Home

Read the Ten Commandments with your family. Choose one commandment and make it the focus of your week. Pray as a family that your choices might reflect faithfulness to that commandment.

What turns us away from God's love?

God created human beings in his image, with intellect and free will, to know and to choose what is true and good. Sin harms our human solidarity and leads to separation and division among individuals, communities, and societies. Choosing to sin and not asking for forgiveness can destroy our relationship with God. Choosing to make a habit of serious sin affects us personally and as a society.

 Go to the digital portal for a prayer of petition.

> "Blessed is the one whose fault is removed,
>   whose sin is forgiven.
> Blessed is the man to whom the LORD imputes
>   no guilt,
>   in whose spirit is no deceit."
>
> *Psalm 32:1–2*

Original Sin is passed down to all people.

The biblical account of Adam and Eve shows how close the relationship between God and human beings was originally. He created them totally free of suffering, anxiety, and shame: "The man and his wife were both naked, yet they felt no shame" (Genesis 2:25).

Everything changed, however, when they chose to turn from God (see Genesis 3). Instead of respecting God's warning and trusting his words, they turned away from God. They selfishly did what *they* wanted, rather than what God commanded. In other words, they committed sin.

This sin of Adam and Eve lost their original holiness and justice. They lost their inner harmony and the peace and friendship they had enjoyed with God, with each other, and with the rest of creation; and their ability to govern themselves with reason, rather than emotions, was impaired.

Faith Word

Original Sin see p. 258

Adam and Eve's personal sin was the first sin. It is called **Original Sin**. Original Sin weakened human nature and brought ignorance, suffering, and death into the world. This wounded human nature has been passed on to the rest of humanity. We all suffer the effects of this first sin, even though we did not personally commit that sin. Sin enslaves us and makes us less free to love and be loved.

God, however, never abandons his people. God promised that a descendant of the first man and woman would save humanity. God promised that sin and evil would one day be overcome.

Activity

What are the effects of Original Sin in the world today? Make a list of examples based on local or national news. Share your list with a partner. How many items did you have in common?

How do I see Original Sin at work in the world?

Did You Know?

God made us for community.

Sin harms human solidarity.

What happens when you throw a stone into a still body of water? When the rock hits the water, it causes ripples to spread out from where it landed. The ripples spread far and wide depending on the size of the stone. You can see the ripples in the pond. Our own freely chosen words and actions have a ripple effect—either for good or bad. What we freely choose to do and say affects others, for good or bad, whether we realize it or not.

Every sin we commit has a ripple effect. It disturbs the unity and harmony that is God's loving plan. God's plan for human society is one of solidarity. Solidarity is a way of living together that supports human dignity, and the material and spiritual goods of all people. But we often cannot see the ripple effect of our sins. Sins that we think are minor or insignificant often have a greater impact than we realize. Sin leads to separation and division among individuals, communities, and even societies. If we could actually see the consequences of our sinful choices on other individuals, on the community, and on society, we might be horrified.

Recall Saint Paul's image of the Body of Christ: "Now you are Christ's body, and individually parts of it" (1 Corinthians 12:27). We are each a part of the Body of Christ. When one part of the Body sins, the other parts are affected. Our sins always reach beyond ourselves. In addition, all sins offend God, because they go against his eternal law.

When we sin against other people, such as with unkind words or deeds, we hurt them. The sin also wounds us. We become less loving toward others and less able to relate to them because we have wronged them. The ripple effect reaches others beyond the people that we have directly harmed, and on and on and on.

One Church, Many Cultures

The Catholic Church in Sri Lanka is dedicated to healing and reconciliation in that country. The Tamil and Sinhalese Catholic communities have adapted to exist within Sri Lanka's mostly Buddhist culture. The Catholic bishops of Sri Lanka dedicated 2017 as the Year of Saint Joseph Vaz, who worked for peace and reconciliation. Saint Joseph lived with people from different ethnic backgrounds and religions. He learned Tamil and Sinhala, the two main languages of the country, so he could speak and work with as many people as possible. The Church in Sri Lanka planned to open a new shrine to Saint Joseph in Colombo. A soup kitchen now stands in his honor, feeding poor schoolchildren in the city.

Pollution is a form of disrespect for God's creation.

Some sins can destroy our relationship with God.

Sin is a destructive force in our world. In the same way that we have the freedom to love God and to do what is good, true, and beautiful, we have the freedom to do the opposite. We have the freedom to choose hate over love, falsehood over truth, and ugliness over beauty.

Mortal sin is sin that destroys charity, the virtue by which we love God above all things and our neighbor as ourselves, in our hearts. To commit a mortal sin, the following conditions need to be met: 1) the sin must be grave (serious), 2) the person committing the sin must have full knowledge of what he or she is doing (that the sin is, in fact, a sin), and 3) the sinner must give full consent of his or her will. In other words, one must choose the sin freely. Mortal sin deprives us of sanctifying grace until we repent and are forgiven through the Sacrament of Penance and Reconciliation.

Faith Word

mortal sin see p. 258

Mortal sin is a grave violation of God's law. It completely turns us away from God. When we commit a mortal sin, we are deliberately and freely choosing to do something that is gravely contrary to God's law.

Sins are evaluated according to their gravity, or seriousness. Mortal sin destroys charity in our hearts. Venial sin offends and wounds charity but does not destroy it.

"If anyone sees his brother sinning, if the sin is not deadly, he should pray to God and he will give him life. This is only for those whose sin is not deadly. There is such a thing as deadly sin, about which I do not say that you should pray. All wrongdoing is sin, but there is sin that is not deadly" (1 John 5:16–17).

Committing sins repeatedly leads to vices, or capital sins.

When we repeat actions, they become habits. A good habit is called a virtue. A bad habit is called a vice. Repeating a sin, even a venial sin, can soon become a bad habit—a vice. This can cause great harm to us personally and to society.

Some vices are called capital sins. The capital sins are pride, avarice (greed), envy, wrath (anger), lust, gluttony, and sloth (laziness). When we are in the bad habit of committing these capital sins, our conscience can become clouded. It is harder for us to know right from wrong and good from evil.

We must always be aware that all sin weakens love. It weakens our ability to love God, ourselves, and others. We shouldn't think of venial sins as "not a big deal." Rather, we must be aware of how easily even small sins, especially when they are repeated, can grow into vices.

Every sin, no matter how "small" or private it may seem, affects us not only personally, but also as a society. As an example, think about gossip. Gossip is when we share a person's faults and failings with others without that person's knowledge. Gossip may be true or false, but it is always harmful to a person's reputation. We can grow accustomed to gossiping about others, and we soon find ourselves in the habit of gossiping face-to-face and online, without thinking

What Makes Us Catholic?

Social media can play an important role in our lives. Pope Francis maintains active social media accounts, but the Church was present on the Internet before his papacy began. The Vatican Web site allows Catholics to learn about Church history and leaders and to explore the Vatican museum collections. Parishes around the world maintain Web sites and social media accounts. Catholic writers, speakers, musicians, men and women religious, and youth leaders share their faith online as well. While we should not allow social media to take too much of our time, the Internet gives us a great opportunity to witness to what we believe.

twice about it! But gossip is a poison that can destroy people's reputations and lives. It also affects the person doing the gossiping. He or she becomes les loving, less kind, and less able to see the world fr another person's viewpoint. Bullying—an inte and repetitive behavior involving the emotio or physical harm of another—is also an e sin that deeply affects both individuals community.

Pope Francis often talks about the sin of gossip.

"Jesus reminds us that words can kill! When we say that a person has the tongue of a snake, what does that mean? That their words kill! Not only is it wrong to take the life of another, but it is also wrong to bestow the poison of anger upon him, strike him with slander, and speak ill of him. . . . gossip can also kill, because it kills the reputation of the person! It is so terrible to gossip! At first it may seem like a nice thing, even amusing, like enjoying a candy. But in the end, it fills the heart with bitterness, and even poisons us. . . . I am convinced that if each one of us decided to avoid gossiping, we would eventually become holy!"

(*Angelus*, February 16, 2014)

Activity

Form groups of four. Have one person read the following story. As it is being read, have one person act the role of Nia (Charles), one act the part of Carolina (Dwayne), and another act the role of David (Monica). Roles have been given alternate names to fit the makeup of your group.

Nia told a false story about a friend, Carolina. Nia thought the story was a funny joke. Word got around, and Carolina got in trouble for something she hadn't done. Carolina was very upset. Another friend, David, learned that Nia had told a false story. David told Nia to pick up a handful of tiny seeds and toss them into the wind and to pick up every single seed before it grew. Nia knew that would be impossible.

After your role-play, discuss as a group how the seeds are like gossip.

Partners in Faith

Saint Basil the Great

Saint Basil the Great lived in what is now Turkey. He spent much ... life preaching against a heresy that said Jesus was not ... man. He encouraged those who wanted to enter ... both on prayer and labor, as well as living ... He spoke out against gossip, or idle ... estroy peace and goodwill.

... out the life of ... Great.

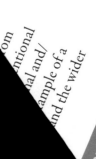

Faith Words

Original Sin   **mortal sin**

 Show What You Know

State whether each statement is true or false by circling the correct answer.
Correct any false statements.

1. Original Sin is the first sin that weakened human nature.

~~True~~   False

_____

_____

2. What we freely choose to do and say does not affect others.

True   ~~False~~

_____

_____

3. Mortal sin damages our friendship with God but does not turn us away from him.

~~True~~   False

_____

_____

Live Your Faith

What would you say to a friend who was about to commit a mortal sin?

_____

_____

_____

_____

_____

How do you avoid the sin of gossip?

_____

_____

_____

_____

_____

_____

Mini-Task

When we talk about people behind their back, we might feel relieved that we are not taking the brunt of the gossip. Or we might feel united in friendship with others doing the gossiping. Pope Francis reminds us that this is "dark joy." Real connection, real friendship, and real joy all come from lifting others up, not tearing them down.

Imagine how you might work with your friends to be a force for good, rather than spreading negativity. Who needs your help or support? How can you join together to do good in your school or community? Use the graphic organizer and tips below to plan how you and your friends will be a Force for Good.

1. *What's going on?* Present an issue of concern about bullying, gossip, or another social issue.

2. *How can you help?*

3. *Suggest* two specific things young people can do.

_____

_____

_____

_____

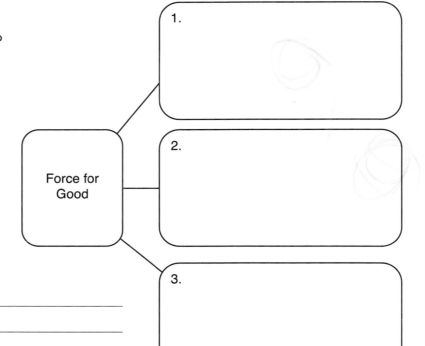

1.

2.

3.

Force for Good

 Want to do more? Go to your Portfolio to continue this activity.

 **At Home**

Talk about your day with your family. How did the actions of family members affect the rest of the family, for good or bad?

What turns us toward God's love?

Throughout salvation history, God has called men and women to share in his life and work. God calls us and gives us the grace to live out our vocation. The Holy Spirit fills us with the free gift of his life. We cooperate with God's plan by our response to his grace and mercy in our lives.

Go to the digital portal for a *Lectio* and *Visio Divina* prayer.

"Remember your compassion and your mercy, O Lord,
for they are ages old.
Remember no more the sins of my youth;
remember me according to your mercy,
because of your goodness, Lord."

Psalm 25:6-7

God invites us to share in his life and work.

The Book of Genesis describes how God first called a man to be the father of his people and to share in his life and work.

God told Abram: "Go forth from your land, your relatives, and from your father's house to a land that I will show you" (Genesis 12:1). God promised to give the land of Canaan to Abram and his descendants forever. As soon as Abram heard God's call, he and his wife, Sarai, did exactly as God had asked. They gathered their family and started the long journey to Canaan.

Abram was 75 years old. He was neither famous nor powerful; his wife, Sarai, could not have children. When God spoke to him, Abram did not argue with God. Rather, Abram had great faith and trusted in God's will.

When Abram and Sarai arrived in Canaan, God told Abram: "Between you and me I will establish my covenant, and I will multiply you exceedingly" (Genesis 17:2). Abram and his descendants would serve God and follow his ways, and God would give Abram a son and make "a great nation" of him (Genesis 12:2). To show that they were beginning a new life as a new people, God changed Abram and Sarai's names to Abraham and Sarah.

God continued to call his people into a covenant relationship with him. Over and over again, God saved his people and called them back to himself.

Centuries after Abraham, God would call a young girl to share in his life and work. Her name was Mary. Mary would say yes to God's grace in her life and become the mother of his divine Son, Jesus Christ, the Savior of the world.

God calls us, too. He invites us to participate in his life and work.

How is God calling me to participate in his work?

Did You Know?

Every life has meaning.

The Annunciation by James Tissot, 1886

God gives us the grace to live out our vocation.

God calls each of us to holiness and eternal life. This is our vocation. How is it possible to live out our vocation? How is it possible to truly live the way God desires us to live in a world filled with challenges and distractions? How is it possible to follow the Ten Commandments, to live Jesus' law of love, to follow the Beatitudes, and to share in God's life and work?

When the angel Gabriel appeared to Mary to announce that she was to bear the Son of God (see Luke 1), she wondered how this could ever come to be. Notice how the angel greeted her. He said: "'Hail, favored one! The Lord is with you'" (Luke 1:28). Mary was God's "favored one" because she was full of grace from the very moment of her Immaculate Conception.

With God's grace, Mary would respond to his call and live out her vocation. And in case Mary had any lingering questions, the angel even reassured her further by saying: "for nothing will be impossible for God" (Luke 1:37). The *Catechism of the Catholic Church* describes it this way: "In the faith of his humble handmaid, the Gift of God found the acceptance he had awaited from the beginning of time. She whom the Almighty made 'full of grace' responds by offering her whole being: 'Behold I am the handmaid of the Lord; let it be [done] to me according to your word'" (*CCC*, 2617).

What Makes Us Catholic?

The word *vocation* comes from *vocare*, which means "to call." A vocation is a call from God. You may have already thought about the work God is calling you to do. This work unites us with Jesus Christ and the Church. There are different states in life to which God may call you to live out your vocation: as a married person, a priest or deacon, a religious sister or brother, or a consecrated layperson. Discovering your vocation involves a process called discernment. Discernment means praying to understand God's plan for you and speaking to people you trust.

Mary wasn't the only one in the Gospels who wondered how she could live out her vocation. When Jesus used the image of a camel passing through the eye of a needle to describe how hard it was for a rich man to enter the Kingdom of God, his dismayed followers asked him: "Who then can be saved?" (Matthew 19:25). He told them: "For human beings this is impossible, but for God all things are possible" (Matthew 19:26).

With God, all things are truly possible. Why? Through Baptism and the other sacraments, God gives us his grace, which is the free and undeserved help we need to follow his commands and live out our vocation. "What God commands he makes possible by his grace" (CCC, 2082). With the help of God's grace, we can, like Mary, say "yes" to God's life in us.

One Church, Many Cultures

Grace is working in an impressive way in the Catholic Church in Africa. It is estimated that by 2025, one-sixth of the world's Catholic population will live on that continent. Many Catholics in Africa are following their vocation and joining religious communities or becoming priests. The largest seminary in the world is in Nigeria, in western Africa. Pope Benedict XVI visited countries in Africa in 2009 and 2011 and celebrated the growing Church there in several meetings and Masses. He said: "In Africa I saw spontaneity in the yes to life, a freshness of the religious sense and of hope."

Activity

You may often be asked what you want to be "when you grow up." Take a few minutes to write about what you would like to do in your future.

_____

_____

_____

_____

_____

_____

_____

Now think about your response above as your vocation from God. Does it make a difference if you think that what you do is God's will for you? Explain your viewpoint.

God freely offers us sanctifying grace.

The free gift of God's life is grace. By "free gift," we mean that none of us can earn grace. Rather, God simply and freely chooses to give us this wonderful gift. The Holy Spirit fills our soul with grace, healing us of our sin and making us holy.

Understanding what this means can be hard. Pope Francis draws on the example of Mary's response to help us understand the power of God's grace. Pope Francis explains that we, like Mary, "have always been 'blessed,' that is, loved. We have been saved thanks to Baptism and to the faith" (*Angelus*, December 8, 2014). **Sanctifying grace**, God's life in us that we receive at Baptism, heals us and makes us holy. How should we respond to this gift? Pope Francis, in the same *Angelus* address, which was on the Solemnity of the Immaculate Conception, gives us an answer:

"Regarding this love, regarding this mercy, the divine grace poured into our hearts, one single thing is asked in return: unreserved giving. Not one of us can buy salvation! Salvation is a free gift of the Lord, a free gift of God that comes within us and dwells in us. As we have received freely, so are we called to give freely . . . If our life is allowed to be transformed by the grace of the Lord, for the grace of the Lord does transform us, we will not be able to keep to ourselves the light that comes from his face, but we will let it pass on to enlighten others."

Faith Word

sanctifying grace see p. 259

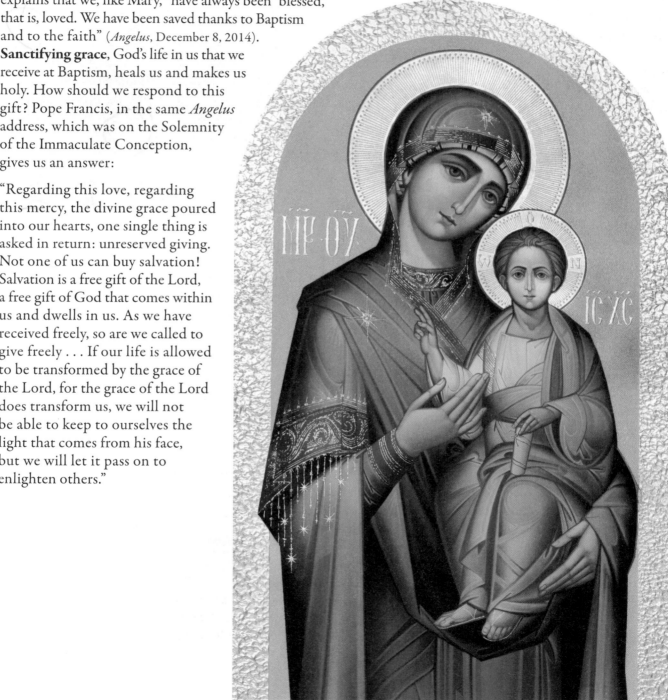

God restores our broken relationships with himself and others after we have sinned.

Faith Word

justification see p. 257

Mary, the Mother of God, more than any other person, shares in God's love because of her response to God's grace and mercy. She "kept her gaze, constantly fixed on the Son and her face became 'the face that looked most like Christ's'" (Dante, *Paradiso*, XXXII, 87). We are each called to this kind of holiness. We are each called, like Mary, to keep our gaze fixed on Jesus. Each of us is called to be the face of Christ in the world. This is possible because we are justified—that is, we are cleansed of sin and reconciled to God.

Justification is the work of God in us, transforming us from sinfulness to holiness. It is God's renovation project for our souls. It restores us to life with him. Justification is granted to us through our Baptism. We receive the gift of sanctifying grace, and our souls are transformed from the state of Original Sin to that of grace. We accept forgiveness and righteousness from God, and we become sons and daughters of God through Christ Jesus. This is all made possible through the Passion, Death, and Resurrection of Christ.

God, in his great mercy, restores our broken relationships. God's work of justification makes us worthy of being united with him. God forgives our sins, makes us holy, and renews our souls. The Holy Spirit makes us whole and holy again. He shares his love and his grace, which helps us turn toward him and away from sin. We respond to his grace and mercy by the way we live. We can be the face of Jesus Christ in the world.

Activity

Sometimes it is hard to keep our eyes on God's grace. Talk with a partner about a time when it was hard to focus on what you believe, and how your faith helped you get your focus back.

Partners in Faith
Blessed Antoine-Frédéric Ozanam

Blessed Antoine-Frédéric Ozanam was a French lawyer, journalist, and professor. Because of his commitment to social justice, he founded what is now known as the St. Vincent de Paul Society. While his faith was central to his life, Blessed Antoine-Frédéric Ozanam knew that his vocation was to be a married man, not a priest. He served God by providing for his family and by caring for those in need in the wider community.

 Learn more about the life of Blessed Antoine-Frédéric Ozanam.

Faith Words

sanctifying grace
justification

 Show What You Know

Circle the correct answer.

1. How would you describe *vocation*?

   a. God's call to obey your parents
   b. God's call to serve him
   c. God's call to take vows

2. What do we call the action of God by which we are freed from sin and reconciled to God?

   a. justification
   b. sanctification
   c. consecration

3. What term describes God's life in us, which we receive at Baptism?

   a. actual grace
   b. spiritual grace
   c. sanctifying grace

Live Your Faith

What vocation interests you? Why?

_____

_____

_____

_____

_____

In what ways have you heard God's call to this vocation?

_____

_____

_____

_____

_____

_____

How do I discern God's call?

Mini-Task

God is at work in our world through the lives and work of people who follow his call. Where do you see God at work? Fill in a job description for someone who wants to do God's work in the world. Include a section on what work a good Christian can do for God.

POSITION AVAILABLE: WORK FOR GOD

REQUIREMENTS:

_____
_____
_____

JOB DESCRIPTION:

_____
_____
_____
_____

TELL US ABOUT YOURSELF:

_____
_____
_____
_____

Want to do more? Go to your Portfolio to continue this activity.

At Home

Talk to others in your family about how they respond to God's grace in their daily responsibilities. What do they think God is calling them to do through their work and interactions with other people?

How do we become what we believe?

Unit 4
The Faith Prayed

The Lord's Prayer

Unit Prayer

Leader: Saint Dominic wanted to be as humble as possible in everything he did, especially in prayer. It is the small, seemingly insignificant things that often matter the most. We must try each day to do whatever we can for God, to become what we believe. If we believe that God loves us, then we show God's love in all we do, even the small things!

Let us listen to how we can become what we believe by doing small things for God. Listen to the stories of missionary disciples among us.

Leader: Let us pray:

Lord Jesus, you taught us to love one another as God loved us. Help us to do this in small, simple things each day. Let our life be a life of praise.

All: Let our life be a life of praise.

Leader: Lord Jesus, you taught us that where two or three are gathered together, you are there. Help us to see you in the faces of those we love and spend time with.

All: Let our life be a life of praise.

Leader: Lord Jesus, you welcomed the stranger and taught us to reach out to those in need. Help us to live as children of God, doing everything for him.

All: Let our life be a life of praise.

(End the Unit Prayer by singing the unit song.)

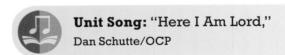

Unit Song: "Here I Am Lord," Dan Schutte/OCP

Missionary Discipleship

What small thing have you done for someone that helped you to live your faith? What small thing have you witnessed someone do for someone else?

What is prayer?

When we pray, we talk with and listen to God. We direct our hearts and minds to him. God has always drawn people to himself in prayer. Prayer is communication between God and his people. We direct our prayers to God, trusting that he hears them.

Go to the digital portal for a prayer of praise.

"If you want to pray better, you must pray more. The more you pray, the easier it becomes. Perfect prayer does not consist of many words but in the fervor of the desire which raises the heart to Jesus."

Saint Teresa of Calcutta

Our hearts and minds are directed toward God in prayer.

At Creation, God called every being from nothingness into existence. Human beings are capable of knowing and experiencing God's love. From the beginning of time, humans have been in search of God. However, God calls us first. He never stops calling each of us to **prayer**. God waits for our prayerful encounter with him, even when we forget about him or turn to idols.

God's love is so faithful and so true that he always takes the first step toward us. Sometimes, though, we do not respond to God's call to enter into a relationship of prayer with him. Yet our God, who is love and who loves us beyond our imagining, is a persistent God. He takes this first step over and over and over again until we respond to his call! The next step is ours: to respond to God's invitation and enter into a prayer relationship with him. When we do this, we lift our minds and hearts to him through prayer, and we ask for the good things we need. We enter into a relationship of love, trust, and friendship.

Faith Word

prayer see p. 258

Pope Francis used the metaphor of inhaling and exhaling to describe a life of prayer. Prayer he said, is like the inhaling of breath: "When we inhale, by prayer, we receive the fresh air of the Holy Spirit" (Address to Catholic Fraternity of Charismatic Covenant Communities and Fellowship, October 31, 2014). The life of prayer enables us to exhale—to share God's love in the world.

Activity

Read Pope Francis' description of prayer in your text. Then stand up, put your hands at your sides, and close your eyes.

As you inhale, imagine the Holy Spirit coming into your heart. As you exhale, say softly: "Lord, let me share your love."

Repeat this prayer three times in honor of the Blessed Trinity.

How has prayer helped me to share God's love in the world?

Pilgrims pray at an evening vigil at the 2016 World Youth Day in Poland.

Did You Know?

The Holy Spirit inspires our prayer.

God has always drawn his people to himself in prayer.

Throughout salvation history, the relationship between God and humanity has been revealed through prayer. The events of the Old Testament, such as those involving Abraham, Samuel, and David, show God always reaching out to his people, calling them into a deeper relationship with him.

Abraham responded to God's invitation to be in a covenant relationship with an attentiveness of the heart that is essential to prayer. He believed in God and walked in his presence. With minds and hearts raised to God, Abraham and Sarah showed wonder and trust that God would give them a son in their old age. Abraham's faith in God remained strong, even when God later asked him to sacrifice his son.

When Samuel was young, God called to him while he was sleeping. At first Samuel thought the priest Eli was calling him. Eli realized that it was God. He told Samuel, "If you are called, reply, 'Speak, LORD, for your servant is listening'" (1 Samuel 3:9). When God called again, Samuel answered. God manifested "himself to Samuel [and] Samuel's word spread throughout Israel" (1 Samuel 3:21). Samuel became God's prophet. A prophet is someone who speaks on behalf of God, reminds people to be faithful to God, defends the truth, and works for justice.

King David was a model of prayer for his people by obeying God's will, praising God, and offering prayers of sorrow and repentance when he sinned. David's prayer expressed a loving and joyful trust in God. Many of the Old Testament Psalms may have been written by David. The psalms can be found in the Liturgy of the Hours, in the Missals, or in the songbooks that we use at Mass.

King David by Matthias Stom, 1633, in a prayerful conversation with God

What Makes Us Catholic?

In Baptism, we are called to share in Christ's role as priest, prophet, and king. As prophets, we speak God's truth and work for justice, just as Christ did. Examples of what some call modern-day prophets include Saint Teresa of Calcutta and Servant of God Dorothy Day. Both women worked for justice for people who were poor or otherwise in need of help. Their faith gave them the strength to speak out and encourage real change in society. These holy women inspire us in our role as prophets today.

Prayer is communication between God and his people.

Moses' relationship with God in prayer shows us that prayer is communication between God and his people. God appeared to Moses from a burning bush. Notice that it is God who begins the conversation:

"There the angel of the LORD appeared to him as fire flaming out of a bush. . . . Although the bush was on fire, it was not being consumed. So Moses decided, "I must turn aside to look at this remarkable sight. Why does the bush not burn up?" When the LORD saw that he had turned aside to look, God called out to him from the bush: Moses! Moses! He answered, "Here I am." God said: Do not come near! Remove your sandals from your feet, for the place where you stand is holy ground. I am the God of your father, he continued, the God of Abraham, the God of Isaac, and the God of Jacob. Moses hid his face, for he was afraid to look at God." (Exodus 3:2–6)

God told Moses that he was to lead his people out of Egypt (see Exodus 3:7–10). Moses was full of doubts and insecurities. "Who am I that I should go to Pharaoh and bring the Israelites out of Egypt?" he asked (see Exodus 3:11).

This event is one of the first images of prayer in the spiritual tradition of both the Jewish people and Christians. God called Moses to be his messenger. Moses did not feel up to the job, yet he eventually learned how to pray in these up-close and personal conversations with God. In his prayers, Moses most frequently asked God to come to the aid of his people. He drew strength from his closeness to God in prayer.

One Church, Many Cultures

The Catholic Church in Ethiopia has a strong connection to the story of Moses and other figures of the Old Testament. The Bible tells us that Moses' wife was Cushite, or what we would now call Ethiopian (see Numbers 12). Over the years, some Ethiopian rulers have claimed they were related to the biblical figures King Solomon and the Queen of Sheba. Some Ethiopian Catholics celebrate and pray using the rites of the Eastern Catholic Churches, while others use the rite of the Roman Catholic (Latin) Church. Liturgies in the southern part of the country include dancing and other sacred movement. Young people make up a large, vocal part of the Catholic Church in Ethiopia.

Moses and the Burning Bush, a Byzantine mosaic at St. Catherine's Monastery, Sinai, Egypt

Prompted by the Holy Spirit, we address our prayers to God the Father, in Christ's name.

The prayers of God's people of both the old and new covenants are primarily addressed to God the Father. In the Old Testament, we find many kinds of prayers. There are prayers of praise, blessing, and thanksgiving, petition, intercession, and sorrow. All of these prayers are addressed to God.

Let's look at some examples of prayers found in the Old Testament. Identify the form of prayer displayed in each of the following passages.

Moses prayed:

"My strength and my refuge is the LORD,
    and he has become my savior.
This is my God, I praise him; the God
    of my father, I extol him."

(Exodus 15:2)

Job prayed:

"The LORD gave and the LORD has taken
    away; blessed be the name of the
    LORD!"

(Job 1:21)

David prayed:

"To you, O LORD, I lift up my soul,
    my God, in you I trust; . . .
Make known to me your ways, LORD;
    teach me your paths."

(Psalm 25:1–2, 4)

Activity

Working independently or with a group, quietly choose one form of prayer: praise, blessing, thanksgiving, petition, or intercession.

In your group, write a psalm based on the form of prayer you chose. Make sure each person in your group gets to write at least one line. When you are finished, share your prayer with the larger group. See if anyone can identify which kind of prayer your group wrote.

Through Moses, God told Aaron to bless the Israelites with these words:

"The LORD bless you and keep you!

The LORD let his face shine upon you, and be gracious to you!

The LORD look upon you kindly and give you peace!"

(Numbers 6:24–26)

In the Gospels, Jesus and God the Father communicate when he prays. Here are a few examples.

- Luke 3:21–22: Jesus prays at his baptism.
- Luke 23:34–46: Jesus prays from his Cross.
- John 11:41–42: Jesus prays at the grave of Lazarus.
- John 12:27–28: Jesus prays before his Passion.

Partners in Faith

Saint Frances Xavier Cabrini

Saint Frances Xavier Cabrini came from a wealthy Italian family. Despite having poor health, she always wanted to be a missionary. She added "Xavier" to her name in honor of Saint Francis Xavier, the patron saint of missionaries. She wanted to go to China, but instead the pope suggested that she go to America to help Italian immigrants. She founded dozens of institutions across America. She is the first U.S. citizen to be canonized a saint.

 Learn more about the life of Saint Frances Xavier Cabrini.

Faith Word

prayer

 ## Show What You Know

Complete the sentences.

1. We call someone who speaks on behalf of God, defends the truth, and works for

   justice a _____.

2. King _____ was a model of prayer for his people.

3. _____ is lifting our minds and hearts to God.

4. The prayers of God's people are primarily addressed to God the _____.

Live Your Faith

Moses sometimes struggled in his work as God's messenger. How does prayer help
you when you are struggling?

_____

_____

_____

_____

_____

_____

_____

_____

God always takes the first step toward us. How do you take the next step toward
him in your prayers?

_____

_____

_____

_____

_____

_____

_____

_____

_____

How and where do I like to pray?

Mini-Task

Communication is an important part of our relationships with friends and family. Communication is also important to our relationship with God. How do you talk with your closest friends? Do you talk with God in the same way?

Use the space on the phone screen to write a conversation between you and God. You can give thanks to God and/or ask God to help you with a challenge you are facing. How is God responding to you?

 Want to do more? Go to your Portfolio to continue this activity.

Think about music that your family finds prayerful and helps you draw closer to God. Play instrumental recordings of that music, if you can. Spend time with your family in prayer as you listen to the music.

Why do we pray?

Throughout salvation history, the prayers of God's people have strengthened their relationship with him. Sacred Tradition teaches that the People of God are a people of prayer. Prayer strengthens our relationship with God and guides us on our journey of faith.

 Go to the digital portal for a prayer of thanksgiving.

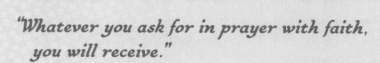

"Whatever you ask for in prayer with faith, you will receive."

Matthew 21:22

Sacred Tradition explains the importance of prayer.

Have you ever had someone, such as a parent, a teacher, or a coach, explain the importance of something you were learning to do? Whether you were learning something brand-new or improving a skill that you had already learned, having someone to teach you and support you would have been very helpful.

Like a trusted parent, teacher, or coach, the Holy Spirit has been with the People of God throughout history, teaching us to respond to the Father in prayer.

In Old Testament times, the People of God prayed at the Temple, led by priests, prophets, and kings. Their prayers reveal **attitudes** of wonder, awe, and reverence before God. In the prophets' prayers, they asked for God's help in times of suffering and persecution. Poets like King David composed the

Faith Word

attitude see p. 257

Psalms. These prayers were the foundation for much of the prayer of Jesus, and they continue to draw members of the Church into prayer today.

In the Old Testament, the New Testament, the lives of saints and other holy men and women, and the Sacred Tradition of the Church, we see the Holy Spirit with God's people, teaching them to pray. From the beginning of salvation history to this very day, people are praying everywhere, all the time, with the help and guidance of the Holy Spirit.

> **How has prayer been a part of my history?**

Did You Know?

 The Church never stops praying.

Prayer strengthens our relationship with God.

When Jesus taught us to pray, he said to begin with the words *Our Father*. We know that this refers to God the Father, but the adjective *our* does not mean that God is a possession. Rather, it expresses a new, close relationship between God and us. Praying the Our Father brings us into communion, or unity, with the Father and with his Son, Jesus Christ.

When we say "our Father," we recognize that God's promises of love and faithfulness announced by the prophets in the Old Testament have been fulfilled in Christ in the New Covenant. God's Kingdom, foretold in the Old Covenant, has come.

Throughout salvation history, God has been at work in the world reconciling humanity to himself, to one another, and to all creation. God has been at work restoring his divine plan that we share in his own life. Through Jesus Christ, we have become adopted sons and daughters of God the Father. We are *his* people— we belong to God. This has been made possible by the grace and truth given to us in the Paschal Mystery of Jesus Christ.

Our prayers bring us closer to God, our Father, and strengthen our relationship with him.

Activity

On the lines below, explain why Jesus told us to begin praying by saying "Our Father."

_____

_____

_____

_____

_____

_____

Constant prayer guides us on our journey of faith.

A consistent thread woven throughout salvation history is this: constant prayer has always guided God's people on their journey of faith, and it continues to do so today. In fact, when we explore Sacred Scripture and read about the lives of the holy men and women of the Old Testament, we find many examples of people who prayed constantly, always seeking God's wisdom and asking for God's help.

Saint Paul said: "Pray without ceasing" (1 Thessalonians 5:17). This means that we should make prayer one of those things that we do constantly, *all the time*. It is always possible to pray—in any place and at any time. Why is it so necessary to pray all the time? Prayer is vitally important for the Christian life. When we do not pray, we can lose our connection with God, falling back into old habits of sin and selfishness. Prayer makes the impossible possible. Prayer allows the Holy Spirit to lead us on our journey of faith.

Praying without ceasing does not mean that we will always feel something when we pray. We will not necessarily always feel that God is near and listening. What about the times when we are so distracted by our own thoughts and everything going on in our lives that we just can't focus when we pray? Or how about the times when it seems that God is distant, even sleeping, and we want to call out: "Hello, God! Are you there?" It is at these very times that we need to continue to pray. Our connection with God will eventually guide us back to our continuing journey of faith.

What Makes Us Catholic?

One way we can focus on our prayers is to always begin prayer with the Sign of the Cross. This gesture is very meaningful. It reminds us that our hearts and minds are devoted to God the Father, the Son, and the Holy Spirit. It also reminds us that we always begin our prayer with reference to the Blessed Trinity. Even when our lives are busy, praying the Sign of the Cross centers our hearts and minds on prayer. The cross is a powerful reminder of God's saving love for us.

> *"Awake! Why do you sleep, O Lord?*
> *Rise up! Do not reject us forever!*
> *Why do you hide your face;*
> *   why forget our pain and misery?"*
>
> Psalm 44:24–25

Across the centuries, the People of God have experienced distractions and dryness in their prayer lives. Many saints and holy people are well known for the difficulties they encountered in prayer. Two of these saints were Saint Teresa of Ávila, who lived in the sixteenth century, and more recently Saint Teresa of Calcutta. They both experienced long periods of emptiness and dryness in prayer. Nevertheless, they kept their hearts focused on God and did not lose their faith. Even the Psalms, the inspired Word of God written long ago, tell us that there will be times when God seems to be hiding from us, or asleep.

Clearly, difficulties and distractions in prayer are not new. They may be even more common for those of us who live in the rapidly changing twenty-first century. As normal as they are, these times of difficulty in prayer challenge us to persevere, to "pray at every opportunity in the Spirit" (Ephesians 6:18).

Activity

Imagine you are a reporter who is investigating the importance of prayer. Interview a friend in your group and ask the following questions.

Do you pray?
How often do you pray?
Where do you pray?
What prayers do you know by heart?
Why is prayer important to you?

Write down the answers and share your report with the group.

One Church, Many Cultures

The biblical King David danced before the Lord (see 2 Samuel 6:14) in prayer, and some psalms suggest dance as a form of prayer (see Psalm 30:12 and Psalm 149:3). In some cultures, dance is an element of communal prayer. For example, Catholics in Chile participate in special sacred dances at a ten-day festival in La Tirana. The festival is a celebration to honor the Virgin Mary. Every July, nearly two hundred thousand people come in colorful costumes to dance in groups. The festival's high point is the Feast of the *Virgen del Carmen* (Our Lady of Mount Carmel) on July 16.

The People of God are a people of prayer.

Someone once said that to become a believer in the power of prayer, there is only one thing a person has to do: start praying. Just ask someone you know who prays regularly what effect prayer has had on his or her life. That person might find it easier to be more loving, especially to those he or she does not particularly like. He or she may experience less temptation to do things that are wrong. That person might face challenges or difficulties with a more positive attitude, or notice more beauty in the world. Those who pray regularly cannot help but notice the effect of prayer on their lives.

The People of God are a people of prayer because *together* we respond to God's invitation to be in a loving relationship with him. For Christians, prayer is a personal response to God—and much more. In Baptism, we become members of Christ's Body, the Church. Our voice joins with the voices of other baptized members of the Church to give thanks and praise to God. Jesus himself told us: "For where two or three are gathered together in my name, there am I in the midst of them" (Matthew 18:20).

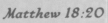

"For where two or three are gathered together in my name, there am I in the midst of them."

Matthew 18:20

Partners in Faith

Saint Francis de Sales

Saint Francis de Sales chose to become a priest, much to the dismay of his wealthy, noble French family. His famous book, *Introduction to the Devout Life*, was unusual for the time— published in 1619—because it was written for laypeople, not priests or nuns. In it, Saint Francis stressed charity over strict penance. He is credited with having written the famous saying "You will catch more flies with a spoonful of honey than with a barrelful of vinegar."

 Learn more about the life of Saint Francis de Sales.

Faith Word

attitude

 ## Show What You Know

Circle the correct answer to complete each sentence.

1. For Christians, prayer is a _____ response to God.

   a. loud
   b. personal
   c. single

2. The _____ were the foundation for much of the prayer of Jesus.

   a. Psalms
   b. Beatitudes
   c. Proverbs

3. The prayers of the People of God revealed _____ of wonder, awe, and reverence before God.

   a. gestures
   b. songs
   c. attitudes

4. Prayer invites the _____ to lead us on our journey of faith.

   a. pope and bishops
   b. Holy Spirit
   c. Bible

Live Your Faith

How do you "pray without ceasing" in your life?

_____

_____

_____

_____

Prayer makes the impossible possible. What "impossible" things would you like to see or feel happen through the power of prayer?

_____

_____

_____

_____

Mini-Task

A podcast is an online audio recording that dives deep into research and exploration of a specific topic. Create your own podcast about prayer. Your podcast could explore why prayer is so important to our faith, or how prayer has an effect on people in their daily lives. Whom could you interview about his or her prayer life? In the space below, write the title of your podcast, the topic for your first show, and the name of the person you will interview.

Prayer Podcast

Title: _____

Topic: _____

Guest: _____

Podcast Script

_____

_____

_____

_____

_____

_____

_____

_____

_____

Want to do more? Go to your Portfolio to continue this activity.

At Home

Talk to your family members about prayer. Discuss how prayer has been important in their lives, and talk about your experiences, too. Talk about the types of prayer that are most helpful to you, and then pray together, using your family's favorite forms of prayer.

How do we pray?

The Holy Spirit teaches the Church to pray. Our daily personal prayer guides our journey of faith. Liturgical prayer deepens our relationship with the Church. All expressions of prayer come from our hearts.

Go to the digital portal for a prayer of intercession.

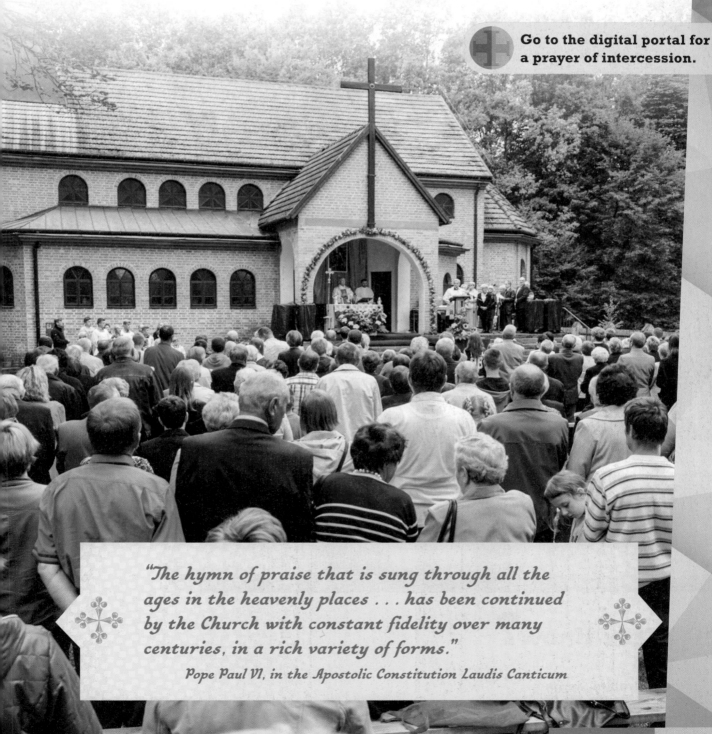

"The hymn of praise that is sung through all the ages in the heavenly places . . . has been continued by the Church with constant fidelity over many centuries, in a rich variety of forms."

Pope Paul VI, in the Apostolic Constitution *Laudis Canticum*

The Holy Spirit teaches the Church to pray.

The Holy Spirit always teaches the Church, reminding us of all that Jesus said and did. With the Holy Spirit's guidance, we are able to pray in a variety of ways. Two of the most common and basic forms of prayer are prayers of petition and prayers of intercession.

In a **prayer of petition**, we ask something of God. This is probably the most common form of prayer. Think about how many times a day we ask God for something. "Help me pass this test!" "Let me know the right thing to say." "Give us good weather for the game today!" "God, forgive me." Asking for forgiveness is the most important type of petition.

We do not need to be shy about asking God for what we need. In fact, Jesus teaches us that his Father is waiting for us to do exactly that:

"And I tell you, ask and you will receive; seek and you will find; knock and the door will be opened to you. For everyone who asks, receives; and the one who seeks, finds; and to the one who knocks, the door will be opened." (Luke 11:9–10).

Faith Words

prayer of petition see p. 258

prayer of intercession
see p. 258

An intercession is a type of petition. When we pray a **prayer of intercession**, we ask for something on behalf of another person or a group of people. Prayers of intercession show our trust in God's care for all people. We pray prayers of intercession at Mass, in the Prayer of the Faithful. We usually pray for the needs of the Church and the salvation of the whole world, for civic leaders, and for those who are suffering or burdened. We may also pray for peace in parts of the world torn by war and strife, for people suffering the ravages of natural disasters, for Christian unity, or for children who are victims of violence. The main thing that all of these examples have in common is that they are prayers for the needs of people all around the world.

Who needs my prayer today?

Did You Know?

Miracles happen.

Saint Peter Preaching, fresco painting by
Masolino da Panicale, 1426

Our daily, personal prayer guides our journey of faith.

The Church never stops praying. And because we are members of the Church, the Church invites us to pray with her all day, every day. We can join with our Church family to pray the Liturgy of the Hours, the daily prayer of the Church. We can participate in Mass on Sunday and, if possible, other days of the week. We can celebrate and pray with the Church throughout all the feasts and seasons of the liturgical year.

The first disciples recognized the importance of both communal and personal prayer (see Acts of the Apostles 2:42–47). We, like the first disciples, gather to worship God and receive the Body and Blood of Christ every Sunday and Holy Day of Obligation when we celebrate Mass. We join together in praise and thanksgiving to God. We pray for one another and for our own needs. We may also pray for the remission, or pardoning, of punishment for our sins and the sins of the souls in Purgatory.

The Church also encourages us to pray on our own. A habit of daily, personal prayer is essential for a Christian disciple. Personal prayer guides our journey of faith and brings us closer to Jesus. Through the power of the Holy Spirit working within us, our prayer connects us to Jesus and nourishes us to spread his Good News everywhere we go.

What Makes Us Catholic?

With your group, you have practiced *Lectio Divina*—praying with Scripture. *Lectio Divina* is a rich and beautiful form of prayer. It includes both meditation and contemplation. You can pray with *Lectio Divina* on your own as well. Follow these steps, each of which is known by its Latin name:

- *Lectio* (reading): read a Scripture passage slowly and with attention.

- *Meditatio* (reflecting): Memorize and silently repeat a word or phrase from the Scripture.

- *Oratio* (responding): Have a prayer conversation with God about that word or phrase.

- *Contemplatio* (resting): Listen for what God has to tell you in prayer.

Activity

Prayers of intercession are a common form of prayer. Write a short prayer of intercession for each of these groups of people:

- Your family

_____

- The poor

_____

- Your Church community

_____

In the liturgy, we join with the Church to worship God.

For centuries, the Church has gathered to pray the liturgy. The prayers of the Church's liturgy are truly some of the most beautiful, awe-inspiring prayers you will ever find. As members of the Body of Christ, we are active participants in this prayer.

In the Church's liturgy, we join with Christ, the Head of the Body, to give praise and thanksgiving to God the Father. This is made possible through the power of the Holy Spirit. We receive God's grace and become more aware of how his grace works in our lives. As a community of believers and as individuals, we become more aware of God's call to us to be faithful disciples of Jesus Christ.

The solemn beginning of the Easter Vigil, when the new fire and Paschal candle are lit, is a beautiful example of liturgical prayer that deepens our relationship with the Church. Before the new fire is lit, the priest instructs the assembly:

"Dear brethren (brothers and sisters),
on this most sacred night,
in which our Lord Jesus Christ
passed over from death to life,
the Church calls upon her sons and daughters,
scattered throughout the world,
to come together to watch and pray.
If we keep the memorial
of the Lord's paschal solemnity in this way,
listening to his word and celebrating his mysteries,
then we shall have the sure hope
of sharing his triumph over death
and living with him in God."

(*Roman Missal*, Easter Vigil)

One Church, Many Cultures

The lighting of the Easter fire and the Paschal candle is an important part of the Easter Vigil celebration. In many European countries, bonfires are lit at dusk on Holy Saturday and burn until dawn on Easter Sunday. In Florence, Italy, Catholics use the Easter fire to light a rocket in the shape of a dove. The dove-shaped firework represents the Holy Spirit and is timed to go off during the singing of the Gloria at Easter Mass.

The priest then blesses the fire, saying with hands extended:

"Let us pray.
O God, who through your Son
bestowed upon the faithful the fire of your glory,
sanctify this new fire, we pray,
and grant that,
by these paschal celebrations,
we may be so inflamed with heavenly desires,
that with minds made pure
we may attain festivities of unending splendor.
Through Christ our Lord.
Amen."

(*Roman Missal*, Easter Vigil)

Then, during the Procession, the Paschal candle is lit. We join together in prayer as the Church. The priest proclaims: "The Light of Christ!" We respond, with great joy: "Thanks be to God!"

Activity

Underline some words or phrases in the Easter Vigil prayer that stand out to you for any reason. Take a few moments to reflect on how the words or phrases make you feel or what they help you understand. You may wish to talk in small groups about your choices.

When we pray, we lift our minds and hearts to God.

Faith Word

psalm see p. 258

All true and genuine prayer, comes from our hearts. Prayer is the lifting of one's mind and heart to God. "Prayer is the life of the new heart" (*CCC*, 2697). Regardless of the expression of prayer—vocal prayer, meditation, or contemplation—all prayer comes from the heart of the person who prays through the inspiration and guidance of the Holy Spirit working within.

The Psalms are a great example of prayer that speaks from the heart. The People of God have prayed the Psalms since they were written. The Book of Psalms, also known as the Psalter, is part of the Old Testament. It is a collection of religious songs that were originally written in Hebrew.

A **psalm** is a poetic prayer designed to be sung or chanted. King David is thought to have written many of the psalms. That would make sense because we know David was a poet and a musician. Other psalms may have been composed by David's son, King Solomon. Still others were written many centuries later.

 Psalm 23

Jesus prayed the psalms often. Today, Jewish people still pray the psalms, and the psalms are also an important part of the liturgical life of all Christians. They help us to pray and to deepen our relationship with God. Psalms are found in the Liturgy of the Hours, part of the official prayer of the Church, and in other prayer books. Psalms are also found in the Missals or songbooks that we use in church, because we sing and pray a Psalm each time we celebrate Mass.

Choose a psalm and pray it. Let your prayer speak from your heart.

Partners in Faith

Saint Catherine of Bologna

Saint Catherine of Bologna lived in Italy in the fifteenth century. She was not very well known during her lifetime, but today she is recognized as the patron saint of artists. Many artists may be able to relate to her creative spirit, talents, visions, and struggle with doubts. The Saint Catherine of Bologna Arts Association in Ringwood, New Jersey, holds an annual photo, art, and poetry exhibition on the weekend closest to March 9, Saint Catherine's feast day. On the six-hundredth anniversary of Saint Catherine's birth, the theme of the festival was "Celebrating the Light That We Are."

 Learn more about the life of Saint Catherine of Bologna.

Faith Words		
prayer of petition	**prayer of intercession**	**psalm**

 Show What You Know

In your own words, write definitions for the terms.

1. psalm

_____

_____

_____

_____

2. prayer of petition

_____

_____

_____

_____

3. prayer of intercession

_____

_____

_____

_____

Live Your Faith

How will you use technology or other reminders to help you make sure you pray every day?

_____

_____

_____

How will you connect to the Church through prayer?

_____

_____

_____

_____

Mini-Task

Authentic prayer is learning how to pause in the middle of our busy days and focus our hearts and minds on the present moment. That moment is a gift from God. One way to slow down is to focus on a single object or activity.

Take a minute to notice something as if for the first time. Pop a piece of candy or a slice of fruit in your mouth and hold it there for one minute. How does it taste? What do you notice about how it feels in your mouth? What does meditating on this piece of food help you realize about the food we eat? How often do you pause to give thanks to God for the little things? Write your thoughts below. Do not worry about putting your thoughts in order—just let them come to you.

_____

_____

_____

_____

What is your experience of God's gift of the present moment?

_____

_____

_____

How can you continue to be mindful of the present moment?

_____

_____

_____

 Want to do more? Go to your Portfolio to continue this activity.

At Home

God's people have prayed the Psalms since ancient times. With your family, find the Book of Psalms in a Bible and choose a psalm to pray. Have family members take turns reading the verses aloud, or simply pray the whole psalm aloud together.

What helps us to pray?

Over the centuries, the Church has been strengthened by different schools of prayer. God's Word, the Church's liturgy, and the virtues of faith, hope, and charity are sources of prayer. We first learn to pray with our families as the domestic church. Faith directs our prayers toward God.

Go to the digital portal for a prayer of praise.

"In times . . . when I am incapable of praying, of practicing virtue, I seek little opportunities . . . to give pleasure to Jesus; for instance, a smile, a pleasant word when inclined to be silent and to show weariness. If I find no opportunities, I at least tell him again and again that I love him; that is not difficult and it keeps alive the fire in my heart."

Saint Thérèse of Lisieux

The Church is strengthened by the witness of saints and holy people.

The saints and others who have come before us and who are already fully in God's Kingdom share with us "the living tradition of prayer by the example of their lives, . . . their writings, and their prayer today" (*CCC*, 2683).

These witnesses are eternally contemplating God, praising him, and caring for those of us on Earth. In fact, they can influence many things: "Well done, my good and faithful servant. Since you were faithful in small matters, I will give you great responsibilities. Come, share your master's joy" (Matthew 25:21). Because they are able to intercede with God on our behalf, we can ask them to advocate for us and for the whole world.

Christian prayer is not "one size fits all" or, in this case, "one prayer style fits all." As we grow in our prayer lives, different expressions of prayer and different spiritual practices can guide us. In fact, a great gift the Church gives us is the richness and diversity of her authentic schools of spiritual tradition,

each of which can guide us on our journey of faith. Many of these have developed from the living tradition of the saints—such as Franciscan (Saint Francis of Assisi), Benedictine (Saint Benedict of Nursia), Carmelite (Saint John of the Cross and Saint Teresa of Ávila), and Ignatian (Saint Ignatius of Loyola). These diverse spiritualties are united by the Holy Spirit in the Church.

Activity

Read about the schools of spirituality below. Circle the one that seems the most interesting to you. Write a few sentences about why it interests you.

Franciscan: centered on embracing a life of simplicity and service; understanding creation as a place we encounter God

Benedictine: a monastic religious life with few possessions and a focus on prayer and personal initiative

Carmelite: focused on one's personal relationship with Christ and deep, contemplative prayer

Ignatian: centered on the process of discernment and a desire to find God in every moment and in all things

What expressions of prayer do I prefer? Why?

Did You Know?

The practice of our faith keeps us faithful.

There are three sources of prayer.

Where does authentic Christian prayer come from? The Holy Spirit is offered to us all the time. The events of each day can make prayer spring from within us. The Holy Spirit is the "living water" in our hearts when we pray. The *Catechism of the Catholic Church* tells us that "there are several wellsprings where Christ awaits us to enable us to drink of the Holy Spirit" (*CCC*, 2652). These sources of prayer are the Word of God, the liturgy of the Church, and the Theological Virtues of faith, hope, and charity.

Through the Word of God, or Sacred Scripture, God reveals himself to us. We can meditate on God's Word and let God speak to us in the quiet of our hearts.

Participating in the liturgy of the Church helps us to pray, most especially through the sacraments. The Church's prayer becomes our prayer. We rest in the presence of God and then go forth to love and serve him.

What Makes Us Catholic?

The Holy Spirit is the "living water," for it is through the Holy Spirit that the waters of Baptism bring about our new life in Christ. Water is so important to our Church that one of the most important sacramentals is holy water. There is a special blessing for holy water when it is blessed outside of a Mass. The priest prays that by the power of the Holy Spirit, the holy water will refresh us "inwardly." He also prays that the holy water will remind us to always live as disciples of Christ. We remember our new life in Christ every time we bless ourselves with holy water. Holy water can also be used to bless our homes and our gardens, as well as friends and family members who are sick. Even our pets can be blessed with holy water!

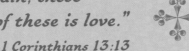
"So faith, hope, love remain, these three; but the greatest of these is love."

1 Corinthians 13:13

With faith, we seek the Lord and hear and keep his Word. Without faith, there would be no reason to pray. With the virtue of hope, we know that God answers our prayers, although sometimes in ways we do not expect. The psalms of the Old Covenant especially teach us to fix our hope on God. Saint Paul taught us that charity, or *love,* is the greatest virtue of all. Love is what motivates us to pray.

"Surely, I wait for the LORD;
who bends down to me and hears my cry."

(Psalm 40:2)

Through the three sources of prayer, we encounter God in the present. We bring prayer into every moment—into the events and situations of each day. We pray for the coming of the **Kingdom of God**, God's reign of peace, justice, and mercy.

Activity

List the three sources of prayer mentioned in your book. Describe each to a friend. Talk about what source of prayer you have experienced the most often. Brainstorm ideas about how you could use all three sources to deepen your relationship with God.

We first learn to pray with our families, as the domestic church.

Recall that the Holy Spirit had come upon the Apostles at Pentecost, and Peter was preaching to the crowds. He preached about Jesus Christ and about repentance and forgiveness of sins (see Acts of the Apostles 2:14–41). Scripture tells us:

"Those who accepted his message were baptized, and about three thousand persons were added that day. They devoted themselves to the teaching of the apostles and to the communal life, to the breaking of the bread and to the prayers. . . . Every day they devoted themselves to meeting together in the temple area and to breaking bread in their homes."

(Acts of the Apostles 2:41–42, 46)

Notice the phrase "every day" in the Scripture passage. The writer of the Acts of the Apostles does not tell us that the first Christian families prayed when they felt like it, or once in a while, or only when there was a crisis. The first Christians prayed *daily*. This wondrous tradition of daily prayer within the family has continued across the centuries, even until today.

From the time of the first Christians, the Holy Spirit has been our teacher in prayer. The Holy Spirit has been present in families, guiding their prayer. Just as those first Christian children learned to pray, centuries ago, we also learn to pray in our families. The family is a church of the home, or a domestic church. We call on the Holy Spirit to be our teacher and guide.

Temple and early Christian village of San Pereto (600–900 AD), Balearic Islands, Spain

Agony in the Garden by Andrea Mategna shows a suffering Jesus. The disciples Peter, John, and James are sleeping. In the background, soldiers led by Judas are already approaching.

Faith directs our prayers toward God.

On the night before Jesus died, he prayed in the company of his Apostles. He knew what would happen to him the next day. There could not have been a more difficult moment for prayer than this moment, one full of desolation and fear of what was to come. Others might have run away.

But Jesus did not run away. Instead, he prayed. He prayed to his Father. Jesus always directed his prayer to God, his Father. The *Catechism* tells us that his

prayer "embraces the whole economy of creation and salvation, as well as his death and Resurrection" (*CCC,* 2746). In this prayer, known as Jesus' priestly prayer, "Jesus reveals and gives to us the 'knowledge,' inseparably one, of the Father and of the Son, which is the very mystery of the life of prayer" (*CCC,* 2751).

Jesus' prayer, like his sacrifice, extends to the end of time. Jesus is the high priest who prays for us and in us. He is "the God who hears our prayer" (*CCC,* 2749). When prayer is difficult, scary, or empty, Jesus is there. He has been there. He knows our struggle. He hears our prayers. When we are distracted and find it hard to pray, Jesus is there, always calling us to him. We pray for the ability to pray in faith with the same determination and courage of Jesus to God, who hears and answers our prayers.

Partners in Faith

Saint Maximilian Kolbe

Saint Maximilian Kolbe died in Auschwitz, a Nazi concentration camp, in 1941. He volunteered to take the place of another man who was about to die. As a young man, Maximilian had a vision of Mary, who offered him the crown of purity or the crown of martyrdom. He chose both. During his final days, Maximilian led a group of his fellow prisoners in prayer. He was the last man of that group to remain alive and was killed with a fatal injection. The man whose life he saved lived to be 94 years old and attended Maximilian's canonization ceremony.

 Learn more about the life of Saint Maximillian Kolbe.

Faith Word

Kingdom of God

 Show What You Know

State whether each statement is true or false by circling the correct answer. Correct any false statements.

1. The Kingdom of God is God's reign of peace, justice, and mercy.

True | False

_____

_____

2. As we grow in our prayer lives, we use the same expressions of prayer and spiritual practices.

True | False

_____

_____

3. Three sources of prayer are the Word of God, the liturgy of the Church, and the Theological Virtues of faith, hope, and charity.

True | False

_____

_____

_____

Live Your Faith

Jesus prayed to God the Father on the hardest night of his life. Have you prayed to God at a difficult time? How did you feel after you prayed?

_____

_____

_____

_____

Which source of prayer is the most helpful to you? Why?

_____

_____

_____

_____

Mini-Task

There are many traditional Catholic prayers that enhance the rich tapestry of our faith. Which is your favorite prayer, and why? In the space below, write your favorite traditional Catholic prayer and then share what you like about this prayer.

My Favorite Prayer

_____

_____

_____

_____

_____

_____

_____

_____

_____

_____

_____

_____

Woman at prayer, part of the East Window at Tudeley Church, Kent, England by Marc Chagall

Teach your favorite prayer to someone who may not know it well.

 Want to do more? Go to your Portfolio to continue this activity.

At Home

Before you go to Mass this Sunday, look up the Scripture readings that will be proclaimed and spend time reading them prayerfully with your family. Tell family members that this will prepare you to understand what God has to say to you in the liturgy.

Why is the Lord's Prayer called the perfect prayer?

The Lord's Prayer is a summary of the whole Gospel. When we pray the Lord's Prayer, we are united to and in communion with God our Father and his Son, Jesus. Praying this prayer shows our respect and love for God and expresses our hope and trust in him.

Go to the digital portal for a *Lectio* and *Visio Divina* prayer.

"The 'Our Father' prayer is the cornerstone of our prayer life. If we are not able to begin our prayer with this word, our prayer will go nowhere."

Pope Francis

When do I pray the Lord's Prayer?

The Lord's Prayer is a summary of the whole Gospel.

The *Catechism of the Catholic Church* tells us that "All the Scriptures—the Law, the Prophets, and the Psalms—are fulfilled in Christ" (*CCC*, 2763). The Gospel is the announcement of the Good News of salvation in Christ promised by God.

The proclamation of this Good News is first summarized in Jesus' teaching in the Sermon on the Mount (see Matthew 5—7). He taught us the Beatitudes and to obey the commandments. He taught about letting go of anger and resentment, about loving our enemies, and about sharing our wealth. Then, right at the very center of this sermon, he teaches about prayer. "This is how you are to pray: Our Father in heaven" (Matthew 6:9). The Lord's Prayer is at the center of Sacred Scripture.

 The Lord's Prayer

In the Sermon on the Mount, Jesus teaches us how to live and how to pray. He gives us lessons on how to live a new life in him, and he also teaches us how to pray to our Father in heaven for this new life. The Lord's Prayer summarizes everything we need in order to live as disciples of Christ. Handed down across the generations, it is the foundation for our life of faith and the most perfect prayer for entering into a conversation with God.

Activity

Write down five things that you think are the most important parts of the Gospel. Link each of your five items to a phrase of the Our Father. Pick one idea from the Gospel and one phrase of the Our Father. How do they affect you in your daily life? Over the next day or two, make an effort to bring these ideas into the ways you think and act.

Did You Know?

 The Lord's Prayer served as a lesson for many of the saints.

In the Lord's Prayer, Jesus invites us into a relationship with his Father.

Long ago, Moses asked God who he was. God replied: "I am who I am" (Exodus 3:14). Through Jesus, we can call God the Father because the Spirit has made him known to us. The depth of this relationship between the Son and the Father is a mystery beyond our complete understanding, yet the Spirit invites all of Jesus' disciples to enter into that very relationship.

The first two words of the Lord's Prayer express the relationship of communion, or unity, that we have with Jesus and God the Father. The words *Our Father* are a blessing of adoration. We recognize God as our Father. We give thanks to him for revealing his name to us, for the gift of believing in him, and for his presence within us. In doing this, we begin to see ourselves differently, because through Christ, we are reborn and restored to God. We are children of God.

Pope Francis described the significance of the Lord's Prayer in this way:

"The entire mystery of Christian prayer is summed up here, in these words: to have the courage to call God by the name 'Father' . . . In fact, calling God by the name 'Father' is by no means something to be taken for granted. . . . Invoking him as 'Father' puts us on a familiar plane with him, as a child turns to his father, knowing that he is loved and looked after by him. When we need help, Jesus does not tell us to resign ourselves and close ourselves off, but rather to turn to the Father . . . who always looks at us with love and who certainly does not abandon us" (General Audience, June 7, 2017).

What Makes Us Catholic?

The *Catechism of the Catholic Church* tells us that early Christian communities prayed the Lord's Prayer three times a day (CCC, 2767). The prayer remains vital to our Church. For example, the Lord's Prayer is an important part of the Church's three Sacraments of Initiation. In Baptism and Confirmation the prayer emphasizes the new life we receive as children of God and as fully initiated members of the Church who have been sealed with the Gift of the Holy Spirit. In the Eucharist, we pray the Lord's Prayer after the Eucharistic Prayer but before receiving Holy Communion. Both the Lord's Prayer and the Eucharist help us to look eagerly toward the fulfillment of the Kingdom of God and the Lord's return in glory.

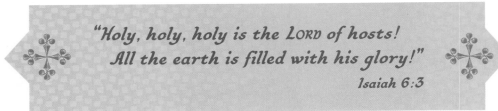

"Holy, holy, holy is the LORD of hosts!
All the earth is filled with his glory!"

Isaiah 6:3

The Lord's Prayer helps us know and honor God.

In the first three petitions of the Lord's Prayer, we give glory to God and pray for the coming of the Kingdom of God. These petitions point us toward God: *thy* name, *thy* kingdom, *thy* will. Notice that we do not mention anything about ourselves in these first three petitions—it is all about God. The *Catechism* describes them this way: "By the three first petitions, we are strengthened in faith, filled with hope, and set aflame by charity" (*CCC*, 2806). In other words, we seek to glorify God and show him both respect and love.

In the first petition, "hallowed be thy name," we ask the Father for help in keeping his name holy.

"O LORD, our Lord,
     how awesome is your name through all
     the earth!"

(Psalm 8:10)

In the Ten Commandments that God gave Moses, God had asked his people to keep his name holy (see Exodus 20:7). This first petition of the Lord's Prayer reminds us that we must honor God's name with deep reverence and awe.

Activity

Write down three things that come to mind when you hear the words *thy kingdom come*.

_____

_____

_____

Invite a friend to share his or her three words. Choose one word that you think best describes what *thy kingdom come* means and write it on a whiteboard. Explain your choice to the whole group.

In the second petition, "thy kingdom come," we pray for the coming of the Kingdom. This was a central theme of Jesus' time on earth. He proclaimed the Kingdom through his words and actions, and, most especially, through his Death and Resurrection. The Kingdom of God is God's reign of justice, peace, and mercy. This petition has a twofold focus. First, it reminds us to help build God's Kingdom today: to be just, peaceful, and merciful people right here and right now. Secondly, it directs us toward the hope of the Kingdom to come at the end of time.

In the third petition, we pray "thy will be done." Our Father's desire is that all people will be saved and come to know the truth. His will for us is summarized in the commandment of Jesus:

"I give you a new commandment: love one another. As I have loved you, so you also should love one another" (John 13:34).

God's will has already been fulfilled in Christ. When we pray "thy will be done," we ask our Father to help us unite our will to Jesus'. This means we pray for grace to do what is pleasing to the Father, as Jesus did. We cannot do this on our own. Only when we are united with Jesus through the power of the Holy Spirit the Father's will be done in us.

In the remaining four petitions of the Lord's Prayer, we ask the Father for what we need. Specifically, we pray that our lives may be nourished and healed of sin, and that we may be victorious in the struggle of good over evil.

One Church, Many Cultures

In some cultures, even people who are not religious remember the Lord's Prayer, so they might pray the words in times of trouble. Before the end of Communism in some Eastern European countries, it was not always safe to practice one's religion. Yet parents and grandparents still shared their faith and prayers with younger people. The Lord's Prayer remained important. The prayer is also familiar to sailors who pray it in times of danger at sea. We do not have to wait for an emergency to pray the Lord's Prayer. The words are always there for us to speak, and God is always there to listen to us.

The Lord's Prayer helps us place our trust in God.

Faith Word

Amen see p. 257

Try to imagine the number of times you have said the word *Amen* over the course of your lifetime. Have you said it one hundred times? Five hundred times? Ten thousand times? Almost every prayer you have ever prayed has ended with **Amen**. It is such a simple word that we use so often. We probably don't think much about its meaning.

Yet, the word *Amen* has powerful significance. It means "so be it." When we say "Amen" at the end of a prayer, we are saying "I believe what I just prayed" or "Let it be so."

Think, then, about what it means to pray "Amen" at the end of the Lord's Prayer. Remember that the Lord's Prayer is the summary of the whole Gospel. When we pray "Amen" at the end of it, we are saying "Yes, I believe in the Gospel message. Yes, let it be so."

Saying "Amen" expresses our commitment to live as children of God and disciples of Jesus. Jesus is the Christ, the Messiah, the one in whom God fulfilled his promise to Abraham and his descendants. All of salvation history has pointed to Jesus. Our "Amen" at the end of the Lord's Prayer expresses our hope and trust in God and his divine plan for us. "The Gospel of Jesus . . . Amen! Yes. I believe and want this to happen in my life."

Partners in Faith

Saint Margaret of Scotland

Saint Margaret was a Scottish queen who helped reform the Church in Scotland. Her kindness and good nature influenced her husband and sons to be good and just rulers. In addition to her royal duties, she attended Mass each day and read frequently from the Bible. She spent much of her time in prayer and in reading. Her husband had her book of the Gospels decorated in jewels. It is now at the Bodleian Library in Oxford, England.

 Learn more about the life of Saint Margaret of Scotland.

Faith	Word

Amen

 ## Show What You Know

Draw a line to match each term to its definition.

1. Our Father

2. Sermon on the Mount

3. the Lord's Prayer

4. Amen

a word that means "so be it"

the most perfect prayer for entering into a conversation with God

a term that is a blessing of adoration for God

Jesus' teaching of how to live and pray

Live Your Faith

What commitment will you express when you say "Amen"?

_____

_____

_____

_____

_____

_____

_____

How will prayer help you work to build God's Kingdom today?

_____

_____

_____

_____

_____

_____

_____

_____

How do I live the will of the Father?

Mini-Task

One of the most important reasons we pray is to keep our lives on the path of discipleship. God has a plan for us and calls us to a life of loving service. While we certainly have free will, prayer helps us remain obedient to God's invitation to help build his Kingdom on earth.

Write about a superhero, a literary figure, or a person you know who models obedience and service to others. How is this person like Christ?

_____

_____

_____

_____

_____

_____

_____

_____

_____

_____

_____

Want to do more? Go to your Portfolio to continue this activity.

At Home

When we say "Amen" at the end of the Our Father, we are saying "Amen! Yes! Make it happen in my life!" With your family, pray the Our Father slowly, including the *Amen.* Talk about things you want to happen in your family's life. After each member of your family has suggested something, say "Amen."

✠ Liturgical Calendar

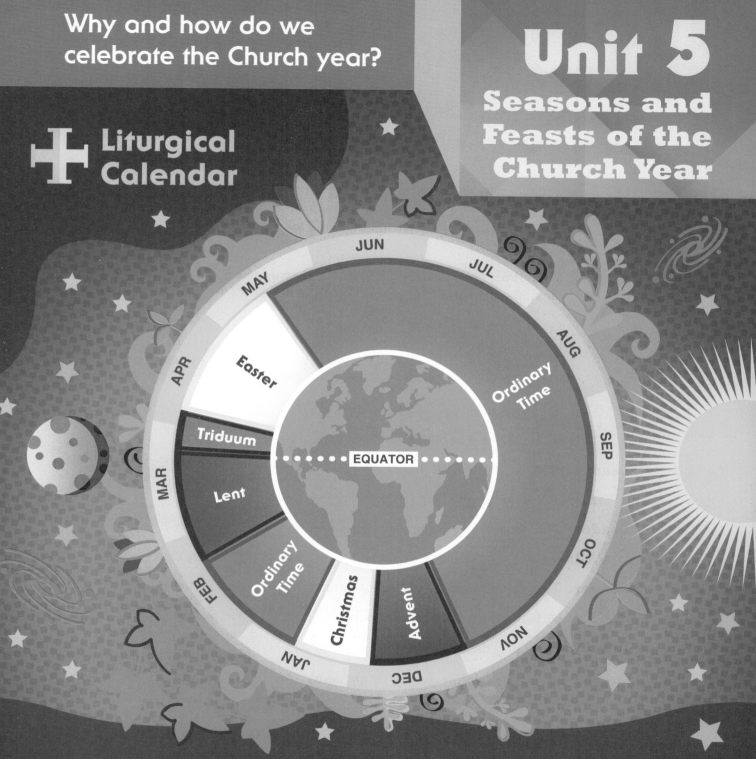

In the liturgical year, the date of Easter Sunday, the celebration of our Lord's Resurrection, depends each year on the spring equinox and the rising of the full moon. Easter Sunday follows the full moon after the spring equinox. The spring equinox is the day on which the sun crosses the equator, making day and night of equal length everywhere. Thus, the timing of Easter Sunday reminds us that our Lord's Resurrection brings light to our darkness.

Astronomers can calculate the date of the spring equinox. Looking at their calculations we find that Easter Sunday is always between March 22 and April 25. Using the date for Easter Sunday, each year's unique liturgical calendar can be determined.

Unit Prayer

Leader: Saint Dominic said: "We must sow the seed, not hoard it."

Through a life of prayer, study, preaching, and community, he believed we would be able to live out the meaning of this prayer. He lived so that others might know and understand God's presence. By doing small things in Christ's name, we can change the world for the better and lead others to Christ.

Let us listen to how others have changed the world by their lives. Listen to the stories of Missionary Disciples.

Let us pray:
Jesus, we learn to sow the seeds of your love through the Mass, the sacraments of the Church, and the saints, whose lives bear witness to their deep faith. For these great gifts, we pray in thanksgiving.

That we hear the call of Jesus to live as a disciple in the world,

All: we long to be your light in the world.

Leader: That we sow the seeds of Christ's love in the world,

All: we long to be your light in the world.

Leader: That we not keep the light of Christ to ourselves,

All: we long to be your light in the world.

Leader: That we reach out in small ways to others,

All: we long to be your light in the world.

Leader: Let us pray the Lord's Prayer. Our Father . . .

(*End the Unit Prayer by singing the song for this unit.*)

Unit Song: "We Are Called,"
David Haas

Missionary Discipleship

When did someone reach out to you when you most needed it? How did it feel? When have your actions shown the light of Christ? How did you feel?

How do we celebrate Jesus Christ?

Church Year

"For I know well the plans I have in mind for you . . . plans for your welfare and not for woe, so as to give you a future of hope."

Jeremiah 29:11

Gathering Prayer

Leader: As disciples of Jesus, we walk in his footsteps through every season and every time. The celebration of the Mass each Sunday is our opportunity to be united with other members of the Body of Christ and to praise and thank God the Father for sending Jesus Christ to save us. The various seasons of the Church year, or liturgical year, allow us to remember and celebrate different aspects of the Paschal Mystery.

May the light of Advent help us prepare a place for the newborn King.

All: We give thanks and praise for the gift of the Church year.

Leader: May the joy of Christmas fill us with peace and hope.

All: We give thanks and praise for the gift of the Church year.

Leader: May the liturgies of Lent and the Easter Triduum offer us a time of reflection, challenge, and conversion.

All: We give thanks and praise for the gift of the Church year.

Leader: May we celebrate the Easter season in gratitude for the gift of the Risen Jesus, who gives us eternal life.

All: We give thanks and praise for the gift of the Church year.

Leader: May Pentecost renew in our hearts the joy and strength of the Holy Spirit.

All: We give thanks and praise for the gift of the Church year.

Leader: In Ordinary Time, may we remember our role as disciples of Christ and listen deeply to the events of Jesus' life during his time on earth.

All: We give thanks and praise for the gift of the Church year.

Activity

Form small groups to take a look at a calendar of the Church year and answer these questions:

What season of the year are we in now?

How long does the current season last?

Which numbered week of the season are we in now?

Who are some saints honored during this season?

The Church year revolves around the events of the Paschal Mystery.

From the beginning of creation, God has had a plan for our salvation. Christ fulfilled this saving plan and continues to offer us salvation until he comes again. The liturgical year celebrates God's saving plan.

The revelation of Jesus is central to the liturgical year. From the birth and childhood of Jesus to his baptism and ministry, and all the way to his Death, Resurrection, and his sending of the Holy Spirit, the events of Jesus' life are told every year in the Church's liturgy.

Key episodes of the account of God's love in the centuries before Christ are also told throughout the liturgical year. Creation, the call of Abraham, the history of Israel, the covenants, and the messages of the prophets are all part of the history of salvation. God works through all of them. We hear these accounts of our ancestors in faith every year in the Liturgy of the Word. They illustrate God's faithfulness in many ways. In particular, they show how all of God's promises were fulfilled in Jesus, the Son.

Finally, the history of the early Church is told in the liturgical year. Every Sunday, we hear a reading from an epistle, or letter, written by an Apostle or other leader of the early Church. These letters explain and interpret the meaning of what God has done. Even though these letters were written to specific early Christian communities, we read their valuable insights as though they were written to us.

In addition, during the Easter season, we hear readings from the Acts of the Apostles. These readings help us to see how God works through the Church to continue the mission of Jesus.

All human beings sin and turn away from God. Yet it has always been God's plan to call us back, with love and forgiveness. The mission of Jesus is to reconcile all of humanity to God the Father. That mission is carried out today through his Church.

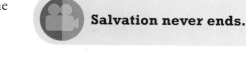

Did You Know?

Salvation never ends.

Church Year

Activity

The Church has cycles of Sunday readings from the Gospels that rotate on a three-year schedule. Cycle A focuses on Matthew. Cycle B focuses on Mark, and Cycle C focuses on Luke. The Gospel of John is read during Lent in Cycle A and in the Easter season in all three cycles. Look in your parish missal or bulletin to find out which cycle we are currently reading.

Work backward to find out which cycle the Church was reading when you were born.

Read the beginning of that Gospel and reflect on what it means to your life.

Readers Theater

Church Year

ROLES:
Jesus, Narrator 1, Narrator 2, Narrator 3,
Narrator 4, Narrator 5, Narrator 6

In the Church year, we remember the life of Jesus during his time here on earth. This passage from Scripture shows how Jesus used parables and stories to teach the people.

Narrator 1: When Jesus addressed the crowds in the Sermon on the Mount, he taught many truths.

Narrator 2: Jesus said: "Stop judging, that you may not be judged. For as you judge, so will you be judged, and the measure with which you measure will be measured out to you" (Matthew 7:1–2).

Jesus: "Why do you notice the splinter in your brother's eye, but do not perceive the wooden beam in your own eye? How can you say to your brother, 'Let me remove that splinter from your eye,' while the wooden beam is in your eye? . . . [R]emove the wooden beam from your eye first; then you will see clearly to remove the splinter from your brother's eye" (Matthew 7:3–5).

Narrator 3: Jesus said: "Ask and it will be given to you; seek and you will find; knock and the door will be opened to you. For everyone who asks, receives; and the one who seeks, finds; and to the one who knocks, the door will be opened" (Matthew 7:7–8).

Jesus: "Which one of you would hand his son a stone when he asks for a loaf of bread, or a snake when he asks for a fish? If you then . . . know how to give good gifts to your children, how much more will your heavenly Father give good things to those who ask him" (Matthew 7:9–11).

Narrator 4: Jesus said: "Do to others whatever you would have them do to you. This is the law and the prophets" (Matthew 7:12).

Narrator 5: Jesus said: "Beware of false prophets, who come to you in sheep's clothing, but underneath are ravenous wolves. By their fruits you will know them" (Matthew 7:15–16).

Jesus: "Just so, every good tree bears good fruit, and a rotten tree bears bad fruit. A good tree cannot bear bad fruit, nor can a rotten tree bear good fruit. Every tree that does not bear good fruit will be cut down and thrown into the fire. So by their fruits you will know them" (Matthew 7:17–20).

Narrator 6: Jesus said: "Everyone who listens to these words of mine and acts on them will be like a wise man who built his house on rock. The rain fell, the floods came, and the winds blew and buffeted the house. But it did not collapse; it had been set solidly on rock" (Matthew 7:24–25).

Jesus: "[E]veryone who listens to these words of mine but does not act on them will be like a fool who built his house on sand. The rain fell, the floods came, and the winds blew and buffeted the house. And it collapsed and was completely ruined" (Matthew 7:26–27).

Narrator 1: The crowds who listened to Jesus were astonished at his teachings.

The Pharisees and the Sadducees Come to Tempt Jesus, James Tissot.

How do I remember and celebrate Christ all year?

Mini-Task

Liturgical celebrations during the Church year take place within an experience of prayer. These celebrations combine Scripture, prayer, music, and reflection. They bring us together with family members, friends, and the wider community, uniting us as one Body of Christ.

For each season of the Church year that you learn about, you are going to outline a simple prayer celebration that young people could participate in during that season.

Consider Scripture, prayer, music, and reflection choices that reflect the different seasons of the Church year. Write your ideas in the planner below.

Church Year Prayer Planner

Liturgical season:

Scripture quote/reading:

Music selection:

Reflection question:

Prayer:

Share your outline with a partner and ask for feedback.

 Want to do more? Go to your Portfolio to continue this activity.

Talk with your family about ways you feel God is inviting you to follow his call. What can each member of your family do to continue Jesus' mission to reconcile the world to God the Father?

Why does Jesus come to save us?

Advent

"*All this took place to fulfill what the Lord had said through the prophet:*
  '*Behold, the virgin shall be with child
   and bear a son,
   and they shall name him Emmanuel,*'
which means 'God is with us.'"

Matthew 1:22–23

Gathering Prayer

Leader: As we celebrate the season of Advent, we thank God for this special time when we prepare to celebrate the birth of Jesus and his return at the end of time.

O God, we wait with patience for your Son, Jesus, and his return at the end of time.

All: We wait with patience and with love for his return.

Leader: We read these words from Isaiah and know that Jesus is the fulfillment of your promises.

"Therefore the Lord himself will give you a sign; the young woman, pregnant and about to bear a son, shall name him Emmanuel" (Isaiah 7:14).

All: We wait with patience and with love for his return.

Leader: "For a child is born to us, a son is given to us;
upon his shoulder dominion rests" (Isaiah 9:5).

All: We wait with patience and with love for his return.

Leader: "They name him Wonder-Counselor, God-Hero,
Father-Forever, Prince of Peace" (Isaiah 9:5).

All: We wait with patience and with love for his return. Amen.

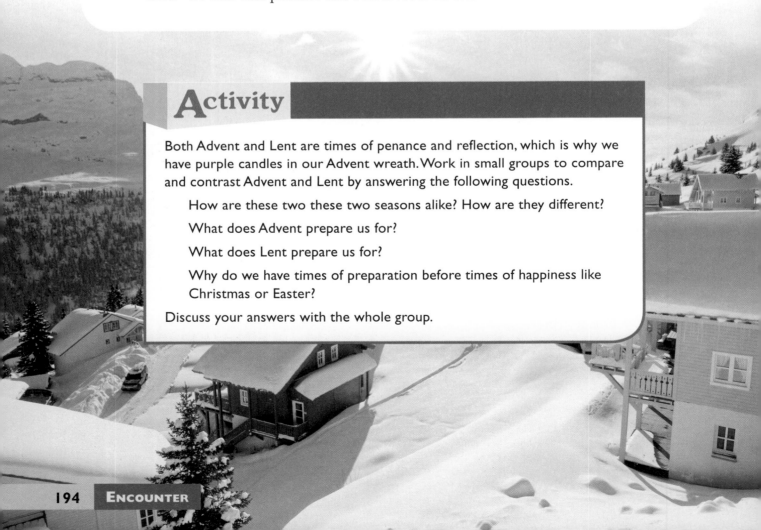

Activity

Both Advent and Lent are times of penance and reflection, which is why we have purple candles in our Advent wreath. Work in small groups to compare and contrast Advent and Lent by answering the following questions.

How are these two these two seasons alike? How are they different?

What does Advent prepare us for?

What does Lent prepare us for?

Why do we have times of preparation before times of happiness like Christmas or Easter?

Discuss your answers with the whole group.

During Advent we anticipate Christ's return in glory.

For many centuries before the coming of Christ, the prophets spoke to God's people about the Messiah, whom God had promised to send. During the liturgies of the Advent season, we hear some key passages from the Bible that describe the prophets' visions. These visions expressed God's plan for the world. The writings of the prophet Isaiah are especially important to the Advent season.

Isaiah used many beautiful images. His prophecies encouraged the people by promising all the good things that would happen when the Messiah came. The world would be at peace, with no more war or hatred. Justice would reign, and truth would triumph over falsehood. The dry land of the desert would be watered and become fruitful. When the Messiah came, people would be healed of their infirmities: the blind would be able to see and the lame would be able to walk.

Jesus is the Messiah who was promised to the Hebrew people. During the Advent season, we pray with the visions of the prophets because through Jesus, God kept his promises. Jesus brings peace and justice. He is the truth. He also brings healing. He opens the eyes of our minds and hearts to see the goodness of God in our world, and he gives us the strength to stand up and do what is right.

God's plan of salvation was fulfilled by Christ's life, Passion, Death, Resurrection, and Ascension. Yet we also look forward to Christ's Second Coming. This is why, each Advent, we listen again to the prophets. Their words renew our hope for the future, when Christ will come in glory.

Did You Know?

Prophets foretold the birth of Jesus.

Activity

Several traditional devotions are prayed during Advent. The O Antiphons are said on the last seven days before Christmas. The first letter of each in Latin, going from last to first, spells the Latin phrase *Ero Cras*, meaning "tomorrow I will come." Learn to say the O Antiphons in Latin and English. Plan to pray them on the days before Christmas. Select two of the O Antiphons, and design a symbol for each of them below.

- December 17: *O Sapientia* (O Wisdom)
- December 18: *O Adonai* (O Lord)
- December 19: *O Radix Jesse* (O Root of Jesse)
- December 20: *O Clavis David* (O Key of David)
- December 21: *O Oriens* (O Dayspring)
- December 22: *O Rex Gentium* (O King of the Nations)
- December 23: *O Emmanuel* (O God with Us)

Advent

Isaiah by Jean Louis Ernest Meissonier, 1838.

Advent Prayer Ritual

"Christ, Circle Round Us,"
Dan Schutte/OCP

Leader: In the name of the Father, and of the Son, and of the Holy Spirit. Amen.

> O come, O come, Emmanuel,
> And ransom captive Israel,
> That mourns in lonely exile here,
> Until the Son of God appear.
> Rejoice! Rejoice! Emmanuel
> Shall come to you, O Israel.

The season of Advent is a time to prepare our minds and hearts for the coming of Christ at Christmas. Let us listen to a reading from Matthew 3:1–3:

In those days, John the Baptist appeared, preaching in the desert of Judea [and] saying, "Repent, for the kingdom of heaven is at hand!" It was of him that the prophet Isaiah had spoken when he said:

"A voice of one crying out in the desert,
'Prepare the way of the Lord,
    make straight his paths.'"

All: Prepare the way of the Lord, make straight his paths.

(Take a few minutes to reflect on the words you have just heard. What words or phrases from the reading stand out to you? Why?)

Leader: Today we will pray with the O Antiphons.

Reader 1: O Wisdom of our God Most High, come to teach us the path of knowledge.

All (sing): Rejoice! Rejoice! Emmanuel shall come to you, O Israel.

Reader 2: O Leader of the House of Israel, come to rescue us with your mighty power.

All (sing): Rejoice! Rejoice! Emmanuel shall come to you, O Israel.

Reader 3: O Root of Jesse's stem, come to save us without delay.

All (sing): Rejoice! Rejoice! Emmanuel shall come to you, O Israel.

Reader 1: O Key of David, come and free those imprisoned by despair.

All (sing): Rejoice! Rejoice! Emmanuel shall come to you, O Israel.

Reader 2: O Radiant Dawn, come and shine on those who dwell in darkness.

All (sing): Rejoice! Rejoice! Emmanuel shall come to you, O Israel.

Reader 3: O King of all nations and keystone of the Church: come and show us the path to peace.

All (sing): Rejoice! Rejoice! Emmanuel shall come to you, O Israel.

Reader 1: O Emmanuel, God dwelling among us: come to save us with your mercy and your might.

All (sing): Rejoice! Rejoice! Emmanuel shall come to you, O Israel.

Leader: Let us offer one another a sign of peace.

Let us sing "O Come, O Come, Emmanuel."

Advent

How do I see Jesus offering salvation to me?

Mini-Task

Advent begins the liturgical year. During the season of Advent, we look forward to celebrating the birth of Jesus at Christmas, and we remember that Jesus will come again.

Outline a prayer celebration for young people for Advent. Consider Scripture, prayer, music, and reflection choices that reflect the Advent season and that would help your community to celebrate Advent. Write your ideas in the planner below.

Advent Prayer Planner

Scripture quote/reading:

Music selection:

Reflection question:

Prayer:

Share your outline with a partner and ask for feedback.

 Want to do more? Go to your Portfolio to continue this activity.

At Home

As a family, talk about areas in your lives where you would like Jesus to bring peace and hope, as the prophets foretold. Pray together that the peace and hope of Jesus will guide your family.

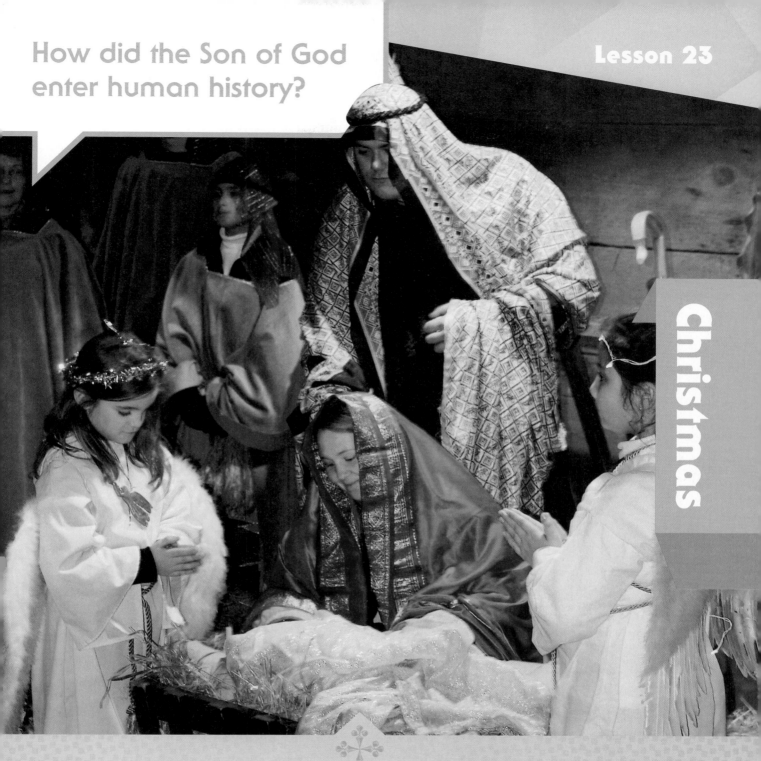

Christmas

"For today in the city of David a savior has been born for you who is Messiah and Lord."

Luke 2:11

Gathering Prayer

Leader: The birth of Jesus at Christmas is one of the most beautiful times in the liturgical year.

We celebrate the love of God poured out in our hearts through the Incarnation of his Son, with accounts from Scripture to tell us how much God loves us. Jesus entered this world as a king born in a humble stable. He wants us to bring his love to the world by sharing his presence with our families, with our friends, and with everyone we meet day to day.

Jesus, Word of God made flesh, help us to see you in the faces of all our sisters and brothers, especially those who are most in need.

All (sing): Hark! The herald angels sing. Glory to the newborn King.

Leader: Jesus, Prince of Peace, teach us how to live a life of peace.

All (sing): Hark! The herald angels sing. Glory to the newborn King.

Leader: Jesus, Light from Light, guide our paths as we seek to bring your light to the world.

All (sing): Hark! The herald angels sing. Glory to the newborn King.

Leader: Jesus, God from God, let your love fill the world this Christmas season and throughout the year.

All (sing): Hark! The herald angels sing. Glory to the newborn King.

Activity

Using the list below, choose one of the witnesses to the birth of Jesus in Luke 2:1–20. Then retell the story as he or she might have experienced it. What did he or she see? Hear? Feel? Share your imaginary experience with the class. Be sure to explain why you chose that person. How did thinking about the Nativity in this way make a difference in what you feel this Christmas?

Witnesses to the Birth of Jesus

Innkeeper • Angel • Shepherd • Wise Man • Townsperson

Christmas celebrates the fulfillment of God's promise to send a Messiah.

Jesus Christ was born at a fixed moment of time in history. Yet Christmas is not only about something that happened long ago in the past. If that were true, then Christmas would be nothing more than a commemoration, like Independence Day or George Washington's birthday.

Of course, it is good to remember the past and to honor events of historical importance. Such remembrances can make us proud or thoughtful about our history. They can help to form our identity. But liturgical celebrations are different. At Christmas, we not only remember the past but also celebrate something that is happening in the present.

The liturgies of Christmas Day often use the word *today*. *Today*, our Savior is born. *Today*, the Lord comes to save us. *Today*, God fills our hearts with joy. This is because the liturgy makes the sacred past part of the present.

The mysteries of Jesus Christ that we celebrate in the liturgy do not simply remain in the past. Rather, in every liturgy, especially the Eucharistic celebration, we participate in the life of the Trinity.

For many centuries before the birth of Christ, God's people hoped and longed for the coming of the Messiah. Jesus Christ is the fulfillment of those hopes and dreams, but in a way that far surpasses anything anyone expected. In fact, the fulfillment of those promises and hopes still continues, as Christ is born to us anew. We continue to hope because Christ is born—today!

Did You Know?

God keeps his promises.

Activity

Work in small groups to describe situations in your lives, at school, and in your community in which you make Christ present to others. What are some effects of Christ's birth you could see occurring in these situations? Write some responses on the lines below.

_____

_____

_____

Christmas Prayer Ritual

 "Hark! The Herald Angels Sing"

Leader: In the name of the Father, and of the Son, and of the Holy Spirit. Amen.

Let us listen to a reading from the Gospel of Luke (2:15–20):

"When the angels went away from them to heaven, the shepherds said to one another, 'Let us go, then, to Bethlehem to see this thing that has taken place, which the Lord has made known to us.' So they went in haste and found Mary and Joseph, and the infant lying in the manger. When they saw this, they made known the message that had been told them about this child. All who heard it were amazed by what had been told them by the shepherds. And Mary kept all these things, reflecting on them in her heart. Then the shepherds returned, glorifying and praising God for all they had heard and seen, just as it had been told to them."

All (sing): O come let us adore him, O come let us adore him, O come let us adore him, Christ, the Lord.

Reader 1: As we stand before the same scene that the shepherds did that night in Bethlehem, let us open our hearts to the Light of Christ, born also to dwell in our hearts.

All (sing): O come let us adore him, O come let us adore him, O come let us adore him, Christ, the Lord.

Reader 2: As Mary held her baby, Jesus, we pray for our own mothers who held us, loved us, and brought us to the saving waters of life so that we, too, might be filled with the light of Christ.

All (sing): O come let us adore him, O come let us adore him, O come let us adore him, Christ, the Lord.

Reader 3: As Joseph knelt by the baby Jesus, we pray for our fathers who love us and help us live as children of God.

All (sing): O come let us adore him, O come let us adore him, O come let us adore him, Christ, the Lord.

Reader 1: As the animals surround the newborn King, let all creation give thanks for this gift of love born for us all.

All (sing): O come let us adore him, O come let us adore him, O come let us adore him, Christ, the Lord.

Leader: Let us offer our own prayers to the newborn King and speak of our gratitude to him. Reflect silently for a moment on the gifts you have received from God. (*pause*) We will now praise and thank our newborn King.

(*Offer your prayer of thanks for God's gifts to you. After all prayers have been offered, pray:*)

All (sing): O come let us adore him, O come let us adore him, O come let us adore him, Christ, the Lord.

The Madonna and Child **by Julius Schnorr Von Carolsfeld, 1885.**

How is Christ a part of my history? How is he part of my life right now?

Mini-Task

During the season of Christmas, we celebrate that God became man in the Incarnation. Celebrating the birth of Jesus should fill us with peace, gratitude, and joy.

Recall what you have learned and experienced about the Christmas season in this lesson. Outline a prayer celebration for young people for Christmas. Consider Scripture, prayer, music, and reflection choices that reflect the Christmas season and that would help your community celebrate. Write your ideas in the planner below.

Christmas Prayer Planner

Scripture quote/reading:

Music selection:

Reflection question:

Prayer: .

Share your outline with a partner and ask for feedback.

 Want to do more? Go to your Portfolio to continue this activity.

 **At Home**

How does your family celebrate Christ *today*? Talk together about a new way you can celebrate Christ and show your hope in him *right now*.

Lent

"Produce good fruit as evidence
of your repentance."

Matthew 3:8

Gathering Prayer

Leader: As we pray during this season of renewal, let us look into our hearts and discover what the Lord Jesus is asking of us. The forty days of Lent help us to look at ourselves more deeply. The liturgies each Sunday contain music and Scripture that help us to consider our own relationship with Jesus and to find the strength to listen to what Jesus is asking of us.

O God, remember your love and your faithfulness.

All: O God, remember your love and your faithfulness.

Leader: Lord God, renew our hearts this Lent as we seek your love and peace.

All: O God, remember your love and your faithfulness.

Leader: Lord God, we turn to you, knowing that we are saved by the Death and Resurrection of Jesus.

All: O God, remember your love and your faithfulness.

Leader: Lord God, we long for your mercy in our lives.

All: O God, remember your love and your faithfulness.

Leader: Lord God, as we walk this journey of Lent, guide us in the loving path of your Son, Jesus.

All: O God, remember your love and your faithfulness.

Activity

Lent is a time when we become closer to Christ. We practice acts of sacrifice, such as giving up candy, doing our chores without being asked, or praying the Rosary instead of playing a video game.

Write down one thing that you will do during Lent to become closer to Christ. You do not need to share with your classmates what you have decided to do.

Lent leads us to a deeper relationship with Christ.

When Jesus went into the desert and fasted for forty days (see Matthew 4:1–11 or Luke 4:1–13), he experienced a test. Going against the First Commandment, Satan tempted Jesus to demonstrate his divinity—his identity as the divine Son of God—in a manner that was contrary to the Father's will. But Jesus did not give in to Satan. He was tested, but he resisted temptation and obeyed his Father's will.

In a symbolic way, the time of testing that Jesus underwent is like the journey of the Chosen People. After God rescued them from slavery in Egypt and brought them through the waters of the Red Sea, they spent forty years in the desert. It was a time of testing. Sometimes the Chosen People wished they could go back to Egypt. Some rebelled against God and set up a golden calf to worship instead. They were tempted to test God and to doubt whether God was really on their side or not.

The Chosen People eventually made it to the Promised Land, however. They looked back on that time of testing as a significant time. It revealed what was really important: being faithful to God and to their calling to be his people.

During the forty days of Lent, when we are tested in our faith, tempted by sin, or attracted to evil, we can rely on the example of Jesus to strengthen us. When we waver, we can turn back to God in the Sacrament of Penance.

The season of Lent can be like a time in the desert as we make sacrifices, pray more earnestly, and give generously to the poor. It can be challenging. But it is also a time to discover (or rediscover) what is really important: being faithful to God and to our calling as people of faith.

Did You Know?

Suffering can strengthen our faith.

Activity

On Ash Wednesday, a sign of the cross is traced on our foreheads with ashes. The ashes come from the blessed palm branches that were used on Palm Sunday the year before. They are burned and saved for the next Lent. Trace a sign of the cross on your forehead. As a group, read the following prayer: "Remember that we are but dust and ashes, yet by God's grace we have died in Baptism and have put on the Lord Jesus Christ" (*Catholic Household Blessings and Prayers*, pages 92–93).

Which part of this prayer is most meaningful to you? Why?

Readers Theater

The Transfiguration

ROLES:
Narrator 1, Narrator 2, Peter,
Jesus, Voice in Cloud

Peter, James, and John went to the top of
a mountain with Jesus.
They were amazed by what they saw there.

Narrator 1: Jesus led Peter, James, and John high up a large mountain. Only the four of them were there. Suddenly Jesus was transfigured and changed dramatically. His clothes became a blazing white. His face changed and shone like the sun.

Narrator 2: At once the prophets Moses and Elijah appeared at each side of Jesus and began talking with him. Peter addressed Jesus.

Peter: "Lord, it is good that we are here. If you wish, I will make three tents here, one for you, one for Moses, and one for Elijah" (Matthew 17:4).

Narrator 1: But as Peter was speaking, a bright cloud cast a large shadow over all of them. And from the cloud came a voice.

Voice: "This is my beloved Son, with whom I am well pleased; listen to him" (Matthew 17:5).

Narrator 2: Hearing the voice, the disciples became terrified and fell to the ground and covered their eyes in fear. But Jesus came to them and touched them, calming them, saying:

Jesus: "Rise, and do not be afraid" (Matthew 17:7).

Narrator 1: When the disciples slowly raised their eyes, they saw no one but Jesus. He was alone. The disciples fell quiet and told no one what they had seen.

The Transfiguration by Carl Heinrich Bloch, 1800s.

How does repentance bring me closer to Christ?

Mini-Task

Lent is a time to focus our thoughts on how we can better live as Christ's disciples. We renew our faith. We get ready to celebrate the wonders of the Paschal Mystery.

Using what you know about Lent, outline a prayer celebration for young people during the season of Lent. Consider Scripture, prayer, music, and reflection choices that reflect the Lenten season and that would help your community to celebrate. Write your ideas in the planner below.

Lent Prayer Planner

Scripture quote/reading:

Music selection:

Reflection question:

Prayer:

Share your outline with a partner and ask for feedback.

 Want to do more? Go to your Portfolio to continue this activity.

Ask each member of your family how Jesus is an example to him or her. What can you do today to show that Jesus is the model for your words and actions?

Why did Jesus die on the Cross and rise again?

Triduum

"*My strength and my refuge is the LORD, and he has become my savior.*"

Exodus 15:2

Gathering Prayer

Leader: The three days of the Sacred Paschal Triduum make up one liturgy that is woven together like a seamless garment. This creates a powerful experience that is unlike any other liturgy of the whole year. Let us answer the call of God to follow the life of Jesus by being his faithful disciples.

We answer the call of God to be faithful disciples.

All: We answer the call of God to be faithful disciples.

Leader: Jesus said to his disciples: "Love one another as I have loved you" (John 13:34).

All: We answer the call of God to be faithful disciples.

Leader: Jesus served his disciples by washing their feet.

All: We answer the call of God to be faithful disciples.

Leader: Jesus gave bread and wine to his disciples and said: "This is my body, which will be given for you; do this in memory of me. . . . This cup is the new covenant in my blood, which will be shed for you" (Luke 22:19–20).

All: We answer the call of God to be faithful disciples.

Leader: Jesus died on the Cross that we might live forever.

All: We answer the call of God to be faithful disciples.

Leader: Jesus rose from the dead, conquering death and the darkness of the world.

All: We answer the call of God to be faithful disciples.

Activity

Spend a few minutes studying a picture of Jesus on the Cross. What are some details you notice? When you are ready, write a Good Friday prayer telling Jesus what his sacrifice means to you. You might use some of the words below to help you.

love   **Savior**   **Body**   **Blood**

_____

_____

_____

_____

_____

The Triduum celebrates Jesus' work of redemption.

The Old Testament accounts of the Chosen People help us understand the Triduum. In particular, the Exodus sheds light on God's plan for salvation. His plan is fulfilled in Jesus and celebrated in the liturgy.

When the Chosen People were getting ready to be led out of slavery, Moses told them to slaughter a lamb and share a meal. He told them to put the blood of the lamb on their doorposts so that the angel of death would "pass over" their houses. The blood of the lamb protected them from physical death. This event, called Passover, is still celebrated by Jews today. It is one of the most important Jewish holidays. This event helps us to understand why we call Jesus the Lamb of God. His blood, shed on the Cross, protects us from eternal death.

The Passover meal prefigures the Eucharist. The dying and rising of Jesus is made present to us today in the celebration of the Eucharist.

When the Chosen People crossed the Red Sea, they rejoiced because God had delivered them from their enemies. By passing through the water, they had passed out of slavery into freedom. The account of the crossing of the Red Sea is always proclaimed at the Easter Vigil. Christians are saved through the water of Baptism.

Did You Know?

The Easter Mysteries are the source of our salvation.

Activity

At the Last Supper, Jesus celebrated the Passover feast with his Apostles. Your text explains that the association of Holy Thursday with Passover is why we call Jesus the "Lamb of God." Talk in small groups about why "Lamb of God" is a fitting title for our Savior.

Readers Theater

The Crucifixion

ROLES:
Narrator 1, Narrator 2, Narrator 3, Pilate,
Crowd, Jesus, Chief priests

*Though Pilate can find no guilt in Jesus, Jesus is
handed over to be crucified.*

Narrator 1: Pontius Pilate was the prefect, or governor, of the Roman province of Judea. Jerusalem was in Judea, and it was the time of the Jewish Passover. It was also a time when Pontius Pilate was in Jerusalem to maintain order.

Narrator 2: Jesus' enemies brought him before the Roman prefect, demanding that Jesus be crucified. Pilate asked the crowd and their leaders why Jesus was brought to him.

Pilate: "Look, I am bringing him out to you, so that you may know that I find no guilt in him" (John 19:4).

Crowd: "Crucify him, crucify him!" (John 19:6)

Narrator 3: Pilate was afraid, because he did not find any guilt in Jesus. He decided to question Jesus himself.

Pilate: "Where are you from?" (John 19:9)

Narrator 1: Jesus did not answer him. So Pilate said:

Pilate: "Do you not speak to me? Do you not know that I have power to release you and I have power to crucify you?" (John 19:10)

Jesus: "You would have no power over me if it had not been given to you from above. For this reason the one who handed me over to you has the greater sin" (John 19:11).

Narrator 2: Pilate took Jesus out to the judges' bench, before the people.

Pilate: "Behold, your king!" (John 19:14).

Crowd: "Take him away, take him away! Crucify him!" (John 19:15).

Chief priests: "We have no king but Caesar" (John 19:15).

Narrator 3: Then Pilate handed Jesus over to be crucified.

Narrator 1: Jesus was made to carry his Cross and walk to the place where he would be crucified. It was called the Place of the Skull. In Hebrew this is called Golgotha.

What is Truth? by Nikolai Nikolaevich, 1890

Narrator 2: Pilate had ordered an inscription placed on the Cross of Jesus. It read: "Jesus the Nazorean, the King of the Jews" (John 19:19). There, on that terrible hill, Jesus was nailed to the Cross and crucified. There were two others being crucified who were on either side of Jesus.

Narrator 3: Standing at the foot of the Cross were his mother, her sister Mary, and Mary of Magdala. As Jesus looked down, he saw his beloved mother and the disciple he loved. Jesus first spoke to Mary, his mother.

Jesus: "Woman, behold, your son" (John 19:26).

Narrator 1: Then Jesus spoke to his disciple.

Jesus: "Behold, your mother" (John 19:27).

Narrator 2: From that moment, the beloved disciple took Jesus' mother into his home. At the very end, Jesus spoke of his thirst, in order that Scripture would be fulfilled. So a sponge soaked in wine was put up to his mouth.

Narrator 3: When Jesus had sipped the wine, he said:

Jesus: "It is finished" (John 19:30).

Narrator 1: With that he bowed his head and handed over his spirit.

How do I pray during the Triduum?

Mini-Task

The Easter Triduum celebrates the Passion, Death, and Resurrection of the Lord, which is the central mystery of the Christian faith. The word *Triduum* means "three days." The Easter Triduum begins at sunset on Holy Thursday and ends at sunset on Easter Sunday. Using what you have learned and experienced about Holy Thursday, Good Friday, Holy Saturday, and Easter Sunday, outline a Triduum prayer celebration for young people. Consider Scripture, prayer, music, and reflection choices that reflect the Easter Triduum and that would help your community to celebrate. Write your ideas in the planner below.

Triduum Prayer Planner

Scripture quote/reading:

Music selection:

Reflection question:

Prayer:

Share your outline with a partner and ask for feedback.

 Want to do more? Go to your Portfolio to continue this activity.

Talk with your family about how each of you will answer the call of God today.

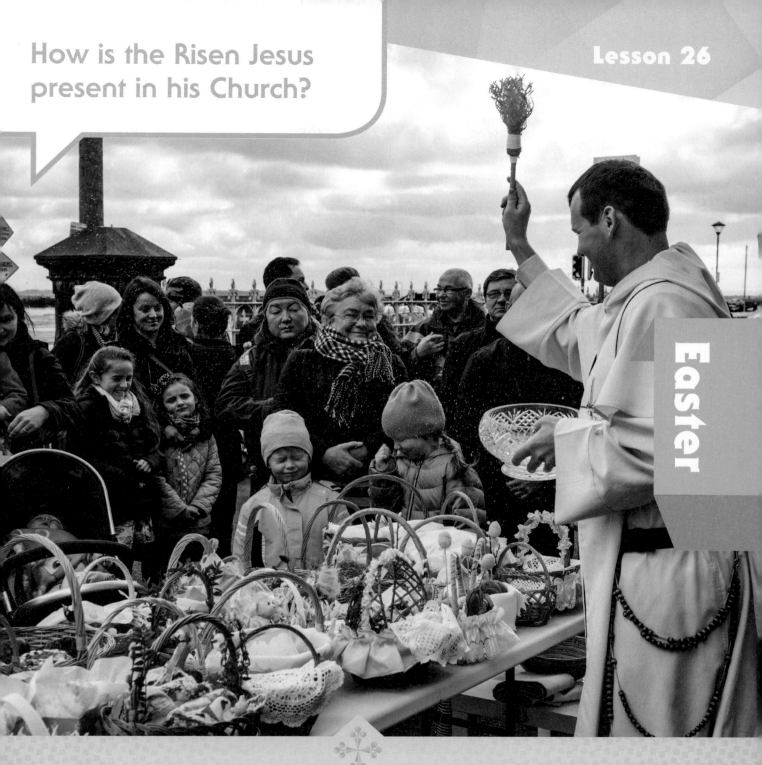

How is the Risen Jesus present in his Church?

Easter

"By the LORD has this been done;
it is wonderful in our eyes."

Psalm 118:23

Gathering Prayer

Leader: During the Easter season, we celebrate the Resurrection of our Lord, Jesus Christ. As members of the Church, we now live in the light of the Risen Lord. We are Easter people!

This is the day that the Lord has made, alleluia.

All: This is the day that the Lord has made, alleluia.

Leader: Risen Jesus, you appeared to your disciples in the upper room sharing your gift of peace and light. We rejoice that we are your disciples.

All: This is the day that the Lord has made, alleluia.

Leader: Let the joy of the Risen Christ be known throughout the world!

All: This is the day that the Lord has made, alleluia.

Leader: Risen Jesus, you were the stranger on the road who was made known to the travelers in the breaking of the bread. Help us to know you in the Eucharist.

All: This is the day that the Lord has made, alleluia.

Leader: Risen Jesus, our hearts are filled with the joy of Easter! Let us celebrate your love in each of us.

All: This is the day that the Lord has made, alleluia.

Leader: Alleluia, alleluia, Christ is risen.

All: This is the day that the Lord has made, alleluia.

Activity

Like the Jewish holiday of Passover, Easter is linked to the cycles of the moon. The early Church decided that the date of Easter would be the first Sunday after the full moon on or after the vernal equinox (which is March 21, the first day of spring). So, Easter can fall anytime between March 22 and April 25. Some people say that we should choose a specific date for Easter, as we do for Christmas. Talk as a group about why we should or should not choose a specific date. Take a group vote on whether you think Easter should fall on a specific date or should continue to depend on the cycles of the moon.

Easter celebrates Jesus' Resurrection and our hope for eternal life in communion with the Blessed Trinity.

Recall that Easter does not last just one day. Rather, Easter lasts for *fifty* days. It is an entire liturgical season in which we can rejoice in the celebration of Christ's Resurrection. Through both personal and communal prayer (and, especially, through the Church's liturgy), we can grow in understanding the meaning of Christ's Resurrection for our own lives of faith.

Psalm 118 is sung often during the Easter season, especially during the first eight days, or octave. This psalm gives thanks to God for his mercy and praises his power. What could be a more perfect example of mercy and power than Jesus being raised from the dead, breaking the hold of sin and death forever?

Written long before the time of Christ, this psalm describes the paradox of the Cross and Resurrection. When Jesus was betrayed and put to death, he experienced complete rejection by the human race. Yet his sacrifice on the Cross and the power of his Resurrection make salvation possible. The psalmist rejoices:

"By the LORD has this been done;
   it is wonderful in our eyes" (Psalm 118:23).

The refrain to Psalm 118 is also deeply meaningful: "This is the day the LORD has made; let us rejoice in it and be glad." Jesus rose from the dead many centuries ago. But this event still brings us great joy and always will.

Did You Know?

All things are possible with God.

Activity

Read the lines from Psalm 118:19–24. Circle the line that applies most to your life right now.

"Open the gates of righteousness;
   I will enter and thank the LORD.

This is the LORD's own gate,
   through it the righteous enter.

I thank you for you answered me;
   you have been my savior.

The stone the builders rejected
   has become the cornerstone.

By the LORD has this been done;
   it is wonderful in our eyes.

This is the day the LORD has made;
   let us rejoice in it and be glad."

Write a few sentences on why this line from the psalm applies to you.

_____

_____

_____

_____

_____

_____

_____

_____

Easter

Easter Prayer Ritual

 "This Is the Day," Tom Kendzia/OCP

Leader: In the name of the Father, and of the Son, and of the Holy Spirit. Amen.

The liturgies of the Easter season are filled with joyful music, and the readings teach us in powerful images about our faith. We especially learn how to live as disciples. One of the most important Gospel accounts of the Risen Jesus is the road to Emmaus, in which Jesus walks along the road with two disciples after his Death and Resurrection. The two disciples do not recognize him, even as they walk and talk about everything that had happened to Jesus over the past few days. Then, the two disciples invite this "stranger" into their home to eat and rest (see Luke 24:13–35).

Reader 1: "And it happened that, while he was with them at table, he took bread, said the blessing, broke it, and gave it to them. With that their eyes were opened and they recognized him, but he vanished from their sight. Then they said to each other, 'Were not our heats burning [within us] while he spoke to us on the way and opened the scriptures to us?'" (Luke 24:30–32).

Reader 2: "So they set out at once and returned to Jerusalem where they found gathered together the eleven and those with them who were saying, 'The Lord has truly been raised and has appeared to Simon!' Then the two recounted what had taken place on the way and how he was made known to them in the breaking of the bread" (Luke 24:33–35).

Reader 3: Let us take a few minutes to reflect on the reading.

As we listen to the song, we will pass around this bread. I invite you to think about the words *They recognized him in the breaking of the bread.*

(*Silent reflection while the song plays.*)

Leader: Why do you think that the two disciples did not recognize Jesus? Why do you think that they finally recognized him in the breaking of the bread? What meaning might this have for us?

Leader: Let us sing "This Is the Day."

(*Sing the song.*)

Leader: Let us offer one another a sign of peace.

In what ways do I bring joy to others?

Mini-Task

Easter is a time of joy and celebration in the Church. We celebrate the Resurrection of Christ and sing "Alleluia" with renewed faith and great rejoicing.

Review the lesson to recall what you learned and experienced about the Easter season. Outline an Easter prayer celebration for young people. Consider Scripture, prayer, music, and reflection choices that reflect the Easter season and that would help your community to celebrate. Write your ideas in the planner below.

Easter Prayer Planner

Scripture quote/reading:

Music selection:

Reflection question:

Prayer:

Share your outline with a partner and ask for feedback.

 Want to do more? Go to your Portfolio to continue this activity.

As a family, talk about something the Lord has done that is "wonderful in your eyes." Offer your thanksgiving to God for his work in prayer.

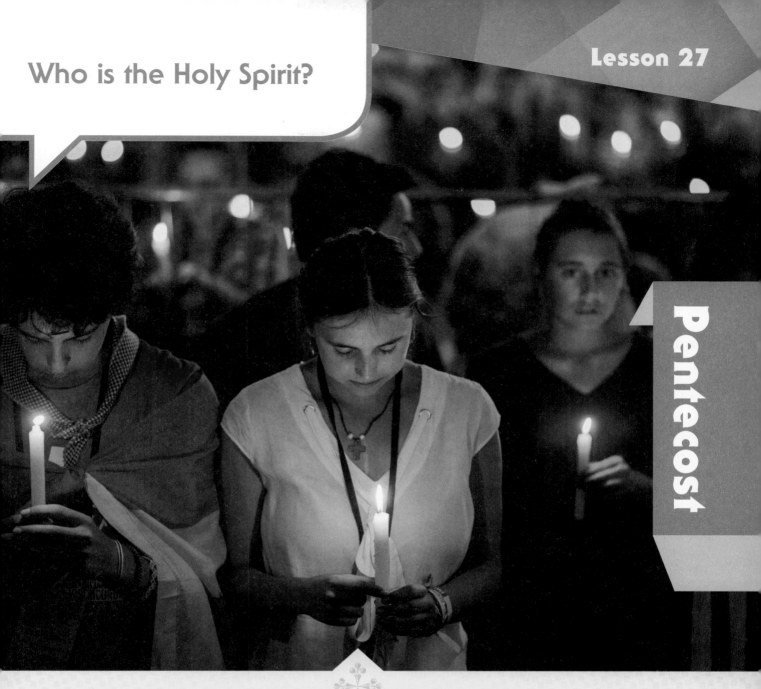

Who is the Holy Spirit?

Pentecost

"Live in a manner worthy of the call you have received . . . striving to preserve the unity of the spirit through the bond of peace: one body and one Spirit."

Ephesians 4:1, 3–4

Gathering Prayer

Leader: On the Solemnity of Pentecost, we celebrate the full revelation of the Church and her mission to spread the Good News of Jesus to all the earth. The Holy Spirit came upon Jesus' disciples, giving them the gifts that they needed to continue Jesus' mission. Let us ask God to send us the Holy Spirit so that we might be faithful disciples and courageous witnesses to the Gospel.

Lord, send us your Spirit. Make us one with you. Fill us with your love and peace.

All: Lord, send us your Spirit.

Leader: O Holy Spirit, send us your gifts so that we can proclaim your love in our words and actions. Give us wisdom, understanding, counsel, and fortitude. Give us knowledge, piety, and fear of the Lord.

All: Lord, send us your Spirit.

Leader: Holy Spirit, come to dwell in us. Help us to be a sign of your love.

All: Lord, send us your Spirit.

Leader: Holy Spirit, guide our lives to follow in the steps of Jesus and to walk in his ways.

All: Lord, send us your Spirit.

Leader: Come, Holy Spirit, come. Fill our hearts with your peace and love, that we might share the love of Christ with everyone we meet.

All: Lord, send us your Spirit.

Activity

Match the gifts of the Holy Spirit to their descriptions.

wisdom	reverence and devotion
understanding	intelligence of the heart
counsel	intelligence of the mind
fortitude	awareness of God
knowledge	strength and courage
piety	wonder at the glory of God
fear (or awe) of the Lord	good judgment

Circle the gift you want most in your life right now.

As Jesus' disciples, we have a mission to proclaim the Good News.

Pentecost Sunday marks the end of the Easter season. This makes our mission clear: We are to be Christ's witnesses in the world, in everything we do. The Good News that Jesus is alive is not just for some people. It is for *everyone*. The Holy Spirit has made us his messengers, so that we might proclaim this truth.

Prompted by the Holy Spirit, the Apostles preached about Jesus. No longer afraid, they were full of joy and hope. Many people heard their message and believed in Jesus. The Holy Spirit came upon these people, too, and many were baptized. On Pentecost Sunday alone, about three thousand people were baptized (see Acts of the Apostles 2:41).

What happened after that first generation of believers? With the Holy Spirit's prompting, they also passed on the Good News to the following generations. The Church continued to grow.

The Holy Spirit works through believers and helps them to become faithful witnesses to Christ. Pentecost does not only celebrate an historical event. Rather, it celebrates the Spirit alive and active in our world and in our hearts today. We are part of this movement. The Holy Spirit will continue to help us to be faithful witnesses until Christ comes again.

Did You Know?

We should prepare to receive God's gifts.

Activity

The fruits of the Holy Spirit are the traits that you show when the Holy Spirit is living within you. They are love, joy, peace, patience, kindness, generosity, goodness, faithfulness, gentleness, modesty, chastity, and self-control. Choose one of these gifts. Then write about why you want to cultivate it in your life.

_____

_____

_____

Share your thoughts with a friend. Together, plan one specific thing you can each do this week with your fruit of the Holy Spirit.

Pentecost Prayer Ritual

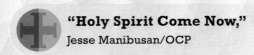

"Holy Spirit Come Now,"
Jesse Manibusan/OCP

Leader: The Solemnity of Pentecost ends the Easter Season and is considered to be the beginning of the public work of the Church. Pentecost reminds us that, as baptized members of the Body of Christ, we are missionary disciples filled with the Spirit of God.

The Solemnity of Pentecost marks our being "sent out into the world" to continue Christ's mission as members of the Church. Let us listen to the account of the first Pentecost.

Reader 1: "When the time for Pentecost was fulfilled, they were all in one place together. And suddenly there came from the sky a noise like a strong driving wind, and it filled the entire house in which they were. Then there appeared to them tongues as of fire, which parted and came to rest on each one of them. And they were all filled with the holy Spirit and began to speak in different tongues, as the Spirit enabled them to proclaim" (Acts of the Apostles 2:1–4).

Leader: Let us take a few minutes to reflect on the reading that we just heard.

(*Silent reflection.*)

Reader 2: How has the Holy Spirit come into your own lives like wind and fire? When have your words or actions been guided by the Holy Spirit?

Leader: Let us listen to the song.

(*Listen to the song.*)

Reader 3: Let us pray:

At our Baptism, we were justified by the grace Jesus earned for us through his Death and Resurrection. Although God chose us and called us by name at our Baptism, we have the free will to choose to follow Christ in our lives. Let us ask the Holy Spirit to dwell in us today and always and to strengthen us to choose Christ.

When we are called to serve one another,

All: I will choose Christ.

Reader 1: When we are asked to love one another,

All: I will choose Christ.

Reader 2: When we are asked to stand up for others who are afraid or are being bullied,

All: I will choose Christ.

Reader 3: Let us come forward to bless ourselves with holy water while singing the song.

(*All sing the song.*)

Leader: Let us offer one another a sign of peace.

How do I share my faith with others?

Mini-Task

Pentecost invites us to respond to the call of discipleship. We celebrate the sending of the Holy Spirit upon the Apostles and disciples to strengthen and encourage them. We remember that we are called to the same mission as they were—to share the Good News of Christ with all the world.

Recall what you have learned and experienced about Pentecost in this lesson. Outline a prayer celebration for young people for Pentecost. Consider Scripture, prayer, music, and reflection choices that would help your community to celebrate. Write your ideas in the planner below.

Pentecost Prayer Planner

Scripture quote/reading:

Music selection:

Reflection question:

Prayer:

Share your outline with a partner and ask for feedback.

 Want to do more? Go to your Portfolio to continue this activity.

At Home

Ask each of your family members to tell one way he or she will be a witness to Christ at home, at school, or at work.

How do we grow as
Jesus' followers?

Ordinary Time

"Blessed are they who hunger and thirst
for righteousness,
for they will be satisfied."

Matthew 5:6

Gathering Prayer

Leader: Ordinary Time is an opportunity for us to learn from Jesus of the love that God has for all of us. Through the many weekends of the two seasons of Ordinary Time, we hear accounts of Jesus' miracles, travels, and teachings. We learn about the many lives that he touched and about his disciples, whom he sent out to teach and heal in his name. We, too, are sent out as his disciples because we are baptized members of his Body. As we gather at Mass each week, we are nourished by Jesus in both Word and sacrament, especially in the Eucharist. Let us open our hearts to the love that Jesus offers us, each and every day.

Leader: Lord Jesus, let our hearts be open to your Word.

All: Lord Jesus, let our hearts be open to your Word.

Leader: Christ Jesus, let our minds be opened by your Word.

All: Christ Jesus, let our minds be opened by your Word.

Leader: Lord Jesus, let our lives be guided by your Word.

All: Lord Jesus, let our lives be guided by your Word.

Leader: Christ Jesus, fill us with your love, grace, and mercy, this day and every day.

All: Christ Jesus, fill us with your love, grace, and mercy, this day and every day.

Activity

During Ordinary Time, we concentrate on our mission of living the Gospel. As the Church, we work on becoming better Christians, not necessarily by doing special things but by doing our everyday, regular activities with more love, compassion, and faith. Create a list of things that you can do during Ordinary Time to deepen your faith and help others. List your top five activities below.

_____

_____

_____

_____

_____

Our models of holiness inspire us to work for the Kingdom of God.

Jesus taught us that happiness is not found through fame or money. We find happiness by living the Beatitudes. Poverty, meekness, mercy, purity of heart, and the longing for justice and righteousness are marks of a Christian. During Ordinary Time, we can grow in living the Beatitudes of God's Kingdom.

The saints are our examples of holiness and of living the Beatitudes. They inspire us. As we celebrate the saints' feast days in the liturgical calendar, we call upon them to help us to be good and faithful Catholics. The saints can support us in our prayer by interceding with God for our own needs and for the needs of the whole world.

Ordinary Time is the longest season in the liturgical year. It is a rich celebration of the events of Jesus' life, his public ministry, and the core of his teachings. When we talk about Ordinary Time, the word *ordinary* does not mean "routine," "normal," or "average." Rather, it comes from the word *ordinal*, meaning "counted time." We count the weeks of

Ordinary Time as we move through the season with ever-deepening love, faith, and commitment to our mission as disciples.

The Church year builds up our practice of prayer by calling us together each Sunday. When we participate in the celebration of the Mass, we are united with people all over the world who celebrate the same liturgy. We are all helping to build the Kingdom of God together, guided by the seasons of the liturgical year. We are also united with the angels and saints—who are part of the heavenly liturgy—as together we offer praise and thanks to God.

Did You Know?

 We can pray for others.

Activity

Many people are named after a saint. That person becomes your patron saint. You can call on your patron when you need help, such as when you are afraid, worried, or need encouragement. Write a prayer that asks your patron saint (or another saint whose life inspires you) to intercede with God for you. The prayers of your patron saint will strengthen your own prayer!

_____

_____

Pray a litany of patron saints with your group.

Readers Theater

The Parable of the Good Samaritan

ROLES:
Narrator 1, Narrator 2, Narrator 3,
Jesus, Lawyer, Samaritan

Jesus tells a story about compassion for others,
whether they are like us or not.

Narrator 1: As Jesus was preaching, there was a lawyer in the crowd who stood up to test Jesus.

Lawyer: "Teacher, what must I do to inherit eternal life? (Luke 10:25).

Narrator 1: Jesus looked at the man and replied:

Jesus: "What is written in the law? How do you read it?" (Luke 10:26).

Lawyer: "You shall love the Lord, your God, with all your heart, with all your being, with all your strength, and with all your mind, and your neighbor as yourself" (Luke 10:27).

Narrator 2: Jesus told the man that he had answered correctly. Jesus added that if the man would do as he just said, he would live a full life. But the lawyer was still testing Jesus, trying to trip him up.

Lawyer: "And who is my neighbor?" (Luke 10:29).

Narrator 3: Jesus begins the parable with a man traveling the dangerous road from Jerusalem to Jericho. It was a road known for harboring vicious robbers.

Jesus: "A man fell victim to robbers as he went down from Jerusalem to Jericho. They stripped and beat him and went off leaving him half-dead" (Luke 10:30).

Narrator 1: Presently, a priest was traveling down the road and came upon the injured man. The priest looked at him and hurried by, making sure to keep to one side of the road.

Narrator 2: Soon after, a Levite, a Jewish man, was also walking down the road and saw the injured traveler. He, too, hurried past on the opposite side of the road.

Jesus: "But a Samaritan traveler who came upon him was moved with compassion at the sight. He approached the victim, poured oil and wine over his wounds and bandaged them. Then he lifted him up on his own animal, took him to an inn and cared for him" (Luke 10:33–34).

Narrator 3: The next day, the Samaritan took out two silver coins and gave them to the innkeeper with instructions.

Samaritan: "Take care of him. If you spend more than what I have given you, I shall repay you on my way back" (Luke 10:35).

Narrator 3: Jesus looked straight at the lawyer.

Jesus: "Which of these three, in your opinion, was neighbor to the robbers' victim?" (Luke 10:36).

Lawyer: "The one who treated him with mercy" (Luke 10:37).

Jesus: "Go and do likewise" (Luke 10:37).

How am I a sign of Christ's love?

Mini-Task

Ordinary Time reminds us of everything we have learned from Jesus. We connect his love and teachings to what we do here and now. We find joy and celebration in the many gifts and blessings of our everyday lives, and we try to share that joy with others.

Outline an Ordinary Time prayer celebration for young people. Consider Scripture, prayer, music, and reflection choices that reflect the season of Ordinary Time and that would help your community to celebrate. Write your ideas in the planner below.

Ordinary Time Prayer Planner

Scripture quote/reading:

Music selection:

Reflection question:

Prayer:

Share your outline with a partner and ask for feedback.

 Want to do more? Go to your Portfolio to continue this activity.

 At Home

Talk with your family about people from the past and the present who help you to be good and faithful Catholics.

Welcome
to your *Christ In Us* Sourcebook

Our Father

Our Father, who art in heaven,
hallowed be thy name;
thy kingdom come;
thy will be done on earth as
    it is in heaven.
Give us this day our daily bread;
and forgive us our trespasses
as we forgive those who
    trespass against us;
and lead us not into
temptation,
but deliver us from evil.
Amen.

Hail Mary

Hail Mary, full of grace,
the Lord is with you!
Blessed are you among women,
and blessed is the fruit of
    your womb, Jesus.
Holy Mary, Mother of God,
pray for us sinners,
now and at the hour of our death.
Amen.

Glory Be to the Father

Glory be to the Father
and to the Son
and to the Holy Spirit,
as it was in the beginning
is now, and ever shall be
world without end.
Amen.

Prayer to Saint Michael the Archangel

Saint Michael the Archangel, defend us in battle;
be our defense against the wickedness and snares
of the devil.
May God rebuke him, we humbly pray;
and do you, O prince of the heavenly host,
by the power of God,
thrust into hell Satan and the other evil spirits
who prowl about the world for the ruin of souls.
Amen.

Gloria

Glory to God in the highest,
and on earth peace to people of good will.
We praise you,
we bless you,
we adore you,
we glorify you,
we give you thanks for your great glory,
Lord God, heavenly King,
O God, almighty Father.
Lord Jesus Christ, Only Begotten Son,
Lord God, Lamb of God, Son of the Father,
you take away the sins of the world,
    have mercy on us;
you take away the sins of the world,
    receive our prayer;
you are seated at the right hand of the Father,
    have mercy on us.
For you alone are the Holy One,
you alone are the Lord,
you alone are the Most High,
Jesus Christ,
with the Holy Spirit,
in the glory of God the Father.
Amen.

Morning Offering

O Jesus, I offer you all my prayers, works,
and sufferings of this day for all the
intentions of your most Sacred Heart. Amen.

Evening Prayer

Dear God, before I sleep
I want to thank you for this day,
so full of your kindness
and your joy.
I close my eyes to rest
safe in your loving care. Amen.

Prayer to the Holy Spirit

Come, Holy Spirit, fill the hearts of your faithful.
And kindle in them the fire of your love.

Send forth your Spirit and they
    shall be created.
And you will renew the face of the earth. Amen.

Jesus Prayer

Lord Jesus Christ, Son of God,
have mercy on me, a sinner. Amen

Apostles' Creed

I believe in God, the Father almighty,
    Creator of heaven and earth,
and in Jesus Christ, his only Son,
    our Lord,
who was conceived by the Holy Spirit,
born of the Virgin Mary,
suffered under Pontius Pilate,
was crucified, died and was buried;
he descended into hell;
on the third day he rose again
from the dead;
he ascended into heaven,
and is seated at the right hand
    of God the Father almighty;
from there he will come to judge
    the living and the dead.
I believe in the Holy Spirit,
    the holy catholic Church,
    the communion of saints,
    the forgiveness of sins,
    the resurrection of the body,
    and life everlasting. Amen.

Canticle of Simeon

"Now, Master, you may let your servant go
    in peace, according to your word,
for my eyes have seen your salvation,
    which you prepared in sight of all the peoples,
a light for revelation to the Gentiles,
    and glory for your people Israel."

(Luke 2:29–32)

Prayer of Saint Dominic

May God the Father, who made us, bless us.
May God the Son, who redeemed us, send healing
    into our midst.
May God the Holy Spirit, who gives us life, move
    within us.

May God give us eyes to see to God, ears to hear God,
and hands to bring God's work into the world.

May we walk with God and preach the word of
    God to all.
May the angel of peace watch over us,
and lead us at last by God's grace to the eternal
    Kingdom.
Amen.

Nicene Creed

I believe in one God,
    the Father almighty,
    maker of heaven and earth,
    of all things visible and invisible.
I believe in one Lord Jesus Christ,
    the Only Begotten Son of God,
    born of the Father before all ages.
    God from God, Light from Light,
    true God from true God,
    begotten, not made, consubstantial
        with the Father;
    through him all things were made.
For us men and for our salvation
    he came down from heaven,
and by the Holy Spirit
    was incarnate of the Virgin Mary,
        and became man.
For our sake he was crucified
        under Pontius Pilate,
he suffered death and was buried,
and rose again on the third day
    in accordance with the Scriptures.
He ascended into heaven
    and is seated at the right hand
        of the Father.
He will come again in glory to judge
        the living and the dead
    and his kingdom will have no end.
I believe in the Holy Spirit, the Lord,
    the giver of life,
    who proceeds from the Father and the Son,
    who with the Father and the Son is
    adored and glorified,
    who has spoken through the prophets.
I believe in one, holy, catholic
    and apostolic Church.
I confess one Baptism for the
    forgiveness of sins
and I look forward to the resurrection of the
    dead and the life of the world to come.
Amen.

Prayer to My Guardian Angel

Angel of God, my guardian dear,
to whom God's love commits me here,
ever this day be at my side,
to light and guard, to rule and guide.
Amen.

The Angelus

V. The Angel of the Lord declared unto Mary,
R. And she conceived of the Holy Spirit.

[say a Hail Mary]

V. Behold the handmaid of the Lord.
R. Be it done unto me according to Your Word.

[say a Hail Mary]

V. And the Word was made flesh,
R. And dwelt among us.

[say a Hail Mary]

V. Pray for us, O holy Mother of God.
R. That we may be made worthy of the promises
of Christ.

Let us pray:

Pour forth, we beseech you, O Lord,
your grace into our hearts;
that as we have known the incarnation of Christ,
your Son by the message of an angel,
so by his Passion and cross
we may be brought to the glory of his Resurrection.
Through the same Christ, our Lord.
Amen.

Divine Praises

Blessed be God.
Blessed be his Holy Name.
Blessed be Jesus Christ, true God and true Man.

Blessed be the Name of Jesus.
Blessed be his Most Sacred Heart.
Blessed be his Most Precious Blood.
Blessed be Jesus in the Most Holy Sacrament of
    the Altar.

Blessed be the Holy Spirit, the Paraclete.
Blessed be the great Mother of God, Mary most Holy.
Blessed be her Holy and Immaculate Conception.
Blessed be her Glorious Assumption.

Blessed be the Name of Mary, Virgin and Mother.
Blessed be St. Joseph, her most chaste spouse.
Blessed be God in his Angels and in his Saints forever.

May the heart of Jesus, in the Most Blessed Sacrament,
be praised, adored, and loved with grateful affection,
at every moment, in all the tabernacles of the world,
even to the end of time,
Amen.

The Canticle of Mary, The Magnificat

"My soul proclaims the greatness of the Lord;
    my spirit rejoices in God my savior.
For he has looked upon his handmaid's lowliness;
    behold, from now on will all ages call me
        blessed.
The Mighty One has done great things for me,
    and holy is his name.
His mercy is from age to age
    to those who fear him.
He has shown might with his arm,
    dispersed the arrogant of mind and heart.
He has thrown down the rulers from their thrones
    but lifted up the lowly.
The hungry he has filled with good things;
    the rich he has sent away empty.
He has helped Israel his servant,
    remembering his mercy,
according to his promise to our fathers,
    to Abraham and to his descendants forever."

(Luke 1:46–55)

Memorare

Remember, most loving Virgin Mary,
never was it heard
that anyone who turned to you for help
was left unaided.
Inspired by this confidence,
though burdened by my sins,
I run to your protection
for you are my mother.
Mother of the Word of God,
do not despise my words of pleading
but be merciful and hear my prayer.
Amen.

Regina Caeli (Queen of Heaven)

Queen of Heaven, rejoice, alleluia:
for the Son whom you merited to bear, alleluia,
is risen, as he said, alleluia.
Pray for us to God, alleluia.

Rejoice and be glad, O Virgin Mary, alleluia!
For the Lord has truly risen, alleluia.

Let us pray. O God, who gave joy to the world
through the Resurrection of your Son, our Lord
Jesus Christ, grant, we beseech you, that
through the intercession of the Virgin Mary, his
Mother, we may obtain the joys of everlasting
life. Through Christ our Lord. Amen.

How to Pray the Rosary

Praying the Rosary creates a peaceful rhythm of prayer during which we can reflect on the mysteries of the Rosary, special times in the lives of Jesus and Mary. Follow the numbered steps to pray the Rosary.

1. Start with the Sign of the Cross.
2. Then pray the Apostles' Creed.
3. Pray an Our Father at every large bead.
4. Pray a Hail Mary at every small bead.
5. Pray a Glory Be to the Father after each set of small beads.
6. Pray the Hail, Holy Queen to end the Rosary.

Mysteries of the Rosary

Joyful Mysteries

1. The Annunciation
2. The Visitation
3. The Birth of Jesus
4. The Presentation of Jesus in the Temple
5. The Finding of Jesus in the Temple

Sorrowful Mysteries

1. The Agony in the Garden
2. The Scourging at the Pillar
3. The Crowning with Thorns
4. The Carrying of the Cross
5. The Crucifixion and Death of Jesus

Glorious Mysteries

1. The Resurrection
2. The Ascension
3. The Descent of the Holy Spirit upon the Apostles
4. The Assumption of Mary into Heaven
5. The Coronation of Mary as Queen of Heaven

The Mysteries of Light

1. Jesus' Baptism in the Jordan
2. The Miracle at the Wedding at Cana
3. Jesus Announces the Kingdom of God
4. The Transfiguration
5. The Institution of the Eucharist

Hail, Holy Queen

Hail, holy Queen, mother of mercy,
hail, our life, our sweetness, and our hope.
To you we cry, the children of Eve;
to you we send up our sighs,
mourning and weeping in this land of exile.
Turn, then, most gracious advocate,
your eyes of mercy toward us;
lead us home at last and show us
the blessed fruit of your womb, Jesus:
O clement, O loving, O sweet Virgin Mary.

1. **sanctuary** the part of the church that includes the altar and the ambo. The word *sanctuary* means "*holy place.*"

2. **altar** the special table that is the center of the celebration of the Liturgy of the Eucharist, also called the Table of the Lord

3. **crucifix** a cross witha figure of Christ crucified, displayed in the sanctuary

4. **tabernacle** the special place in the church in which the Most Blessed Sacrament is placed in reserve

5. **sanctuary lamp** light or candle that is always lit near the tabernacle. It helps us to remember that Jesus is really present in the Most Blessed Sacrament.

6. **ambo** a sacred reading stand called the Table of the Word of God. The ambo is used only for proclamation of the Scripture in the Liturgy.

7. **chalice** the special cup into which the proest pours grape wine that becomes the Blood of Christ during the Liturgy of the Eucharist

8. **paten** the special plate on which the priest places the wheat bread that becomes the Body of Christ during the Liturgy of the Eucharist

9. **cruets** small glass jars that contain the water and the grape wine used at Mass

10. **presider's chair** chair on which the priest who is celebrating Mass sits

11 processional cross cross with a figure of Christ crucified that is carried in the entrance procession and may also be carried during the Offertory procession and during recessional

12 Paschal candle a large candle that is blessed and lit every Easter. The lighted Paschal candle represents the Risen Christ among us. The flame of the Paschal candle is used to light baptismal candles.

13 baptismal font or pool contains the water that is blessed and used during the Sacrament of Baptism

14 Stations of the Cross fourteen pictures that help us to follow the footsteps of Jesus during his Passion and Death on the Cross

15 Reconciliation Room or confessional a separate space for celebrating the Sacrament of Penance and Reconciliation. This is where you meet the priest for individual confession and absolution. You may sit and talk to him face-to-face or kneel behind a screen.

16 stained glass colorful windows that may show saints or scenes from Scripture

17 pews where the assembly is seated during the celebration of Mass

18 statue of Mary image of the Mother of God, our greatest saint. Statues of other saints may also be found in the church.

Celebrating the Mass

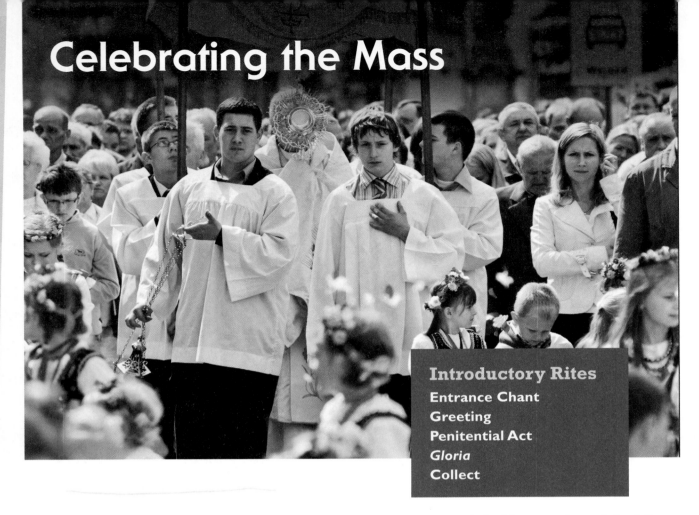

Introductory Rites
Entrance Chant
Greeting
Penitential Act
Gloria
Collect

Do you and your family sometimes wonder what the Mass is really all about? Here is a simple guide that brings awareness to the greatest prayer of the Catholic Church—the celebration of the Eucharist, or Mass.

Take a closer look at how the Mass begins and ends and at the two parts of the Mass—the Liturgy of the Word and the Liturgy of the Eucharist. All our prayers of praise and thanksgiving form one single act of worship. Share the meaning of these sacred moments with your family.

We Gather. . .

What better way to begin our worship than with an entrance song and a procession of the priest and other ministers! This shows our unity, for together we are the Body of Christ—the Church—gathered in God's name. Watch as the priest and deacon kiss the altar and bow. It is on the altar, the table of the Lord, that the sacrifice of Christ is made present. We remember and make present the work of

salvation accomplished by Jesus through his life, Death, Resurrection, and Ascension into heaven.

Together we pray, "In the name of the Father, and of the Son, and of the Holy Spirit." God is with us. In God's presence, we confess that we are not perfect; we have sinned. We pray for God's mercy and ask for the prayers of the community and all the saints. In this way, we prepare ourselves—mind, heart, and soul—to participate in the sacred mysteries of the Mass.

On most Sundays, we pray an ancient hymn called the *Gloria*, first sung by the angels at the birth of Christ: "Glory to God in the highest . . . / For you alone are the Lord, / you alone are the Most High, / Jesus Christ, / with the Holy Spirit, / in the glory of God the Father." This hymn of praise speaks of the mystery of the Trinity, the Triune God, in whose name we gather.

The priest then prays the Collect, the opening prayer that expresses the theme of the celebration and the needs and hopes of the assembly.

Liturgy of the Word

God placed in each of our hearts a desire to know him better. At Mass we are invited to actively listen to the Word of God. In Scripture, God speaks to us of the wonders of salvation and of his love for all creation. Yet God also has a special message for each individual who hears his holy Word. What might that be for you or for members of your family?

Our response after listening to the First Reading, usually from the Old Testament, and the Second Reading, from the New Testament, is "Thanks be to God." God's Word is not merely a collection of past events. God continues to act in our lives today; his word has the power to transform us.

Between these readings is the Responsorial Psalm, which can be spoken or sung. Jesus himself prayed the psalms, which express every kind of emotion, as well as what we desire from God. The psalms are beloved prayers of the Bible in which we ask the Lord for many things, such as insight, renewal, guidance, strength, and protection.

Our dialogue with God continues as we prepare to encounter Christ in the Gospel. Now, though, we are standing, singing *Alleluia*, or other words of praise. Standing is a sign of honor for the Gospel, the Good News of Jesus Christ. This is the high point of the Liturgy of the Word. Jesus Christ, our Savior, speaks to us—comforting, strengthening, and calling us to live as his disciples. As the priest or deacon introduces the Gospel (Matthew, Mark, Luke, or John) our bodies are at prayer, too. We trace the sign of the cross on our forehead, lips, and heart. In this way, we ask that God's Word be in our thoughts, in the words we speak, and in our hearts, taking root and moving us to praise and bless the Lord and to do good in the world.

The homily that follows is to help us understand what God's Word means and reminds us that we are not alone. God's Word is within us, guiding us, and leading us to worship. The whole assembly then prays the Creed, stating aloud what we believe as members of the Church. In the Universal Prayer we pray for the needs of all God's people.

Liturgy of the Word
First Reading
Responsorial Psalm
Second Reading
Gospel Acclamation
Gospel
Homily
Profession of Faith
Universal Prayer

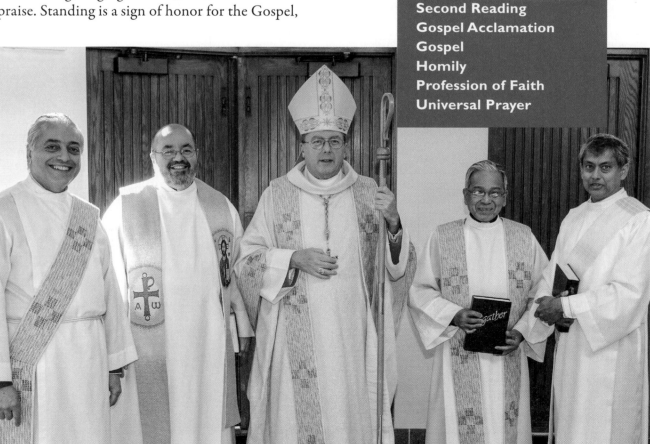

Liturgy of the Eucharist

At the heart of the entire liturgical celebration is the Liturgy of the Eucharist. It begins with the Presentation of the Gifts of bread and wine and a Prayer over the Offerings. This is a symbolic expression of joining ourselves with the sacrifice of Christ. We should offer not only what is positive in our lives, but also our struggles and sorrows. In essence, we unite our whole selves—everything we are and hope to be—with the sacrifice of Christ.

Now is the time for the high point of the entire celebration—the Eucharistic Prayer. We are on our knees, in quiet reverence. The priest, in our name, thanks God for all his works of salvation. Our resounding response of praise is: "Holy, Holy, Holy Lord God of hosts. / Heaven and earth are full of your glory."

We have come to the very heart of the Mass—the changing of the bread and wine into the Body and Blood of Christ. What a beautiful mystery of faith. Jesus is our high priest, and Jesus is present on the altar under the appearances of bread and wine. This is what makes the celebration of Mass the "perfect" act of worship. Jesus is offering the sacrifice through the ministry of the priest and is the one being offered. Listen. You can hear Jesus' words, as the Apostles' heard so long ago: "THIS IS MY BODY, WHICH WILL BE GIVEN UP FOR YOU . . . THIS IS THE CHALICE OF MY BLOOD . . . WHICH WILL BE POURED OUT FOR YOU AND FOR MANY FOR THE FORGIVENESS OF SINS." By the power of the Holy Spirit, our gifts of bread and wine have become the very Body and Blood of the risen Christ.

Jesus is truly present, even though the appearances of bread and wine remain. We prepare to receive Christ so that he may work in us. Together we pray the Lord's Prayer that Jesus taught us. We pray that Christ's peace be with us always. We offer one another a sign of peace to show that we are united in Christ.

With your family, watch as the priest breaks the consecrated bread, the Body of Christ. Jesus also made this gesture–the Breaking of the Bread–at the Last Supper. It shows our unity, for in Holy Communion, we share in the one bread that is broken for us all. When we receive Holy Communion with faith and love, Christ can help us to become better, to become more patient and forgiving, with a greater love and compassion for other people.

Liturgy of the Eucharist
Presentation of the Gifts
Prayer over the Offerings
Eucharistic Prayer
Communion Rite
  Lord's Prayer
  Rite of Peace
  Breaking of the Bread
  Holy Communion

We Go in Peace . . .

In the Concluding Rites, the priest offers a final prayer and blesses us in the name of the Father, the Son, and the Holy Spirit. We hear these or other words of dismissal: "Go in peace, glorifying the Lord by your life." The Mass doesn't really end; it is meant to continue in our daily lives.

How will you and your family bring Christ to the world?

Concluding Rites
Greeting
Blessing
Dismissal

Stations of the Cross

In the Stations of the Cross, we follow in the footsteps of Jesus during his Passion and Death on the Cross.

1 Jesus is condemned to die.
2 Jesus takes up his Cross.
3 Jesus falls the first time.
4 Jesus meets his mother.
5 Simon helps Jesus carry his Cross.
6 Veronica wipes the face of Jesus.
7 Jesus falls the second time.

8 Jesus meets the women of Jerusalem.
9 Jesus falls the third time.
10 Jesus is stripped of his garments.
11 Jesus is nailed to the Cross.
12 Jesus dies on the Cross.
13 Jesus is taken down from the Cross.
14 Jesus is laid in the tomb.

Celebrating the Sacrament of Penance and Reconciliation

Individual confession

First, I examine my conscience.
The priest greets me.
We both make the Sign of the Cross.

The priest asks me to trust in God's mercy.
The priest or I may read from Scripture.

I talk with the priest and I confess my sins.
The priest talks to me about loving God and others.
He gives me an act of penance.
I pray an Act of Contrition.

In the name of God and the Church, the priest grants me absolution.
The priest extends his hand over my head.
I receive God's forgiveness of my sins through the words and actions of the priest.

Together, the priest and I give thanks for God's forgiveness.
I am sent to go in peace and to do the penance the priest gave me.

The Ten Commandments

1. I am the LORD your God: you shall not have strange gods before me.

2. You shall not take the name of the LORD your God in vain.

3. Remember to keep holy the LORD's Day.

4. Honor your father and your mother.

5. You shall not kill.

6. You shall not commit adultery.

7. You shall not steal.

8. You shall not bear false witness against your neighbor.

9. You shall not covet your neighbor's wife.

10. You shall not covet your neighbor's goods.

The Great Commandment

"You shall love the Lord, your God, with all your heart, with all your soul, and with all your mind. This is the greatest and the first commandment. The second is like it: You shall love your neighbor as yourself."

Matthew 22:37–39

The New Commandment

"I give you a new commandment: love one another. As I have loved you, so you also should love one another. This is how all will know that you are my disciples, if you have love for one another."

John 13:34–35

The Beatitudes

"Blessed are the poor in spirit,
for theirs is the kingdom of heaven."

"Blessed are they who mourn,
for they will be comforted."

"Blessed are the meek,
for they will inherit the land."

"Blessed are they who hunger and thirst for righteousness,
for they will be satisfied."

"Blessed are the merciful,
for they will be shown mercy."

"Blessed are the clean of heart,
for they will see God."

"Blessed are the peacemakers,
for they will be called children of God."

"Blessed are they who are persecuted for the sake of righteousness, for theirs in the kingdom of heaven."

The Seven Sacraments

The Sacraments of Christian Initiation
Baptism
Confirmation
Eucharist

The Sacraments of Healing
Penance and Reconciliation
Anointing of the Sick

The Sacraments at the Service of Communion
Holy Orders
Matrimony

The Power of Grace

How do we live as disciples of Jesus? Through the power of God's grace, we can grow in our friendship with God. Grace is a share in God's life and love. We receive grace at our Baptism and when we receive the other sacraments. The water of Baptism is a sign of the life that God gives us through his grace. Throughout our lives, grace helps us respond to God with love. It gives us the strength to live as Jesus' disciples.

Precepts of the Church

The pope and bishops have established some laws to help us know and fulfill our responsibilities as members of the Church. These laws are called the Precepts of the Church.

It is helpful to think of the precepts as rules or principles intended as a guide for behavior. They teach us how we should act as members of the Church. These precepts also make sure that the Church has what it needs to serve its members and to grow.

1. You shall attend Mass on Sundays and Holy Days of Obligation and rest from servile labor.

2. You shall confess your sins at least once a year.

3. You shall receive the Sacrament of the Eucharist at least during the Easter season.

4. You shall observe the days of fasting and abstinence established by the Church.

5. You shall help to provide for the needs of the Church.

Holy Days of Obligation

Each Sunday of the liturgical year is a great celebration of the Church, or a solemnity. In addition to each Sunday, there are other solemnities in the liturgical year on which we are obliged to attend Mass to give special honor to Jesus Christ for the salvation he has given to us. These are called Holy Days of Obligation. Post this list of holy days in your home to remind everyone of them!

- **Solemnity of Mary, Mother of God** (January 1)

- **Ascension** (when celebrated on Thursday during the Easter season*)

- **Assumption of Mary** (August 15)

- **All Saints' Day** (November 1)

- **Immaculate Conception** (December 8)

- **Christmas** (December 25)

   Some dioceses celebrate the Ascension on the following Sunday.

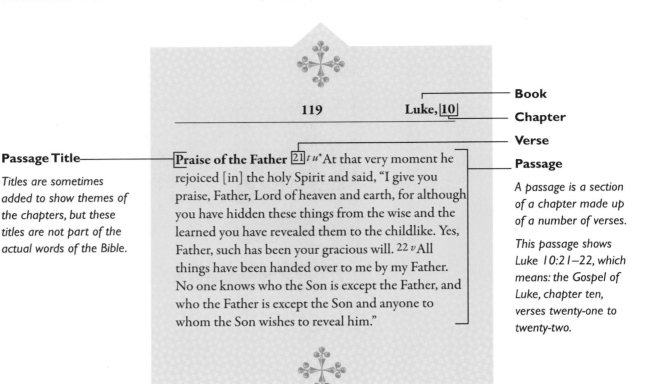

Passage Title

Titles are sometimes added to show themes of the chapters, but these titles are not part of the actual words of the Bible.

Book

Chapter

Verse

Passage

A passage is a section of a chapter made up of a number of verses.

This passage shows Luke 10:21–22, which means: the Gospel of Luke, chapter ten, verses twenty-one to twenty-two.

Content within image:

119   Luke, 10

Praise of the Father 21 *t u* *At that very moment he rejoiced [in] the holy Spirit and said, "I give you praise, Father, Lord of heaven and earth, for although you have hidden these things from the wise and the learned you have revealed them to the childlike. Yes, Father, such has been your gracious will. 22 *v* All things have been handed over to me by my Father. No one knows who the Son is except the Father, and who the Father is except the Son and anyone to whom the Son wishes to reveal him."

Reading the Bible . . . in Five Easy Steps

When you are given a Scripture passage to read, here are five easy steps that will help you to find it! With your child, follow these steps to look up **Lk 10:21–22**.

1. **Find the book.** When the name of the book is abbreviated, locate the meaning of the abbreviation on the contents pages at the beginning of your Bible. *Lk* stands for Luke, one of the four Gospels.

2. **Find the page.** Your Bible's contents pages will also show the page on which the book begins. Turn to that page within your Bible.

3. **Find the chapter.** Once you arrive at the page where the book begins, keep turning the pages forward until you find the right chapter. The image above shows you how a chapter number is usually displayed on a typical Bible page. You are looking for chapter **10** in Luke.

4. **Find the verses.** Once you find the right chapter, locate the verse or verses you need within the chapter. The image above also shows you how verse numbers will look on a typical Bible page. You are looking for verses **21** and **22**.

5. **Start reading!**

Your *Christ In Us*
Family Companion

Welcome. We are so glad that you are a ***Christ In Us*** family. In this section, you will find a treasury of resources as your family accompanies your child on our journey to a greater love in Jesus Christ. This material is written specifically for you as adult family members. But be certain that you review your child's resources that precede this section. Also, don't forget to look over the *Glossary* that follows. It will give you a good overview of what your child has been experiencing this year. Finally, the *Q&A* offers a wonderful opportunity for your entire family to review the major faith statements of the grade.

The Books of the Bible

The word "Bible" comes from the Greek word *biblia*, which means "books." Most of the books of the Old Testament were originally written in Hebrew, and the books of the New Testament in Greek. In the fifth century, a priest and scholar named Saint Jerome translated the books of the Bible into Latin, the common language of the Church at the time. Saint Jerome also helped to establish the *canon*, or the Church's official list of the books of the Bible. Many centuries later, in 1384, the first English translation of the Bible was completed.

The chart below lists the sections and books of the Bible. It also shows abbreviations commonly given for the names of the books in the Bible.

Old Testament

Pentateuch ("Five Scrolls")

These books tell about the formation of the covenant and beliefs of the Israelites.

Genesis (Gn)
Exodus (Ex)
Leviticus (Lv)
Numbers (Nm)
Deuteronomy (Dt)

Historical Books

These books deal with the history of Israel.

Joshua (Jos)
Judges (Jgs)
Ruth (Ru)
1 Samuel (1 Sm)
2 Samuel (2 Sm)
1 Kings (1Kgs)
2 Kings (2 Kgs)
1 Chronicles (1 Chr)
2 Chronicles (2 Chr)
Ezra (Ezr)
Nehemiah (Neh)
Tobit (Tb)
Judith (Jdt)
Esther (Est)
1 Maccabees (1 Mc)
2 Maccabees (2 Mc)

Wisdom Books

These books explain God's role in everyday life.

Job (Jb)
Psalms (Ps)
Proverbs (Prv)
Ecclesiastes (Eccl)
Song of Songs (Song)
Wisdom (Wis)
Sirach (Sir)

Prophetic Books

These books contain writings of the great prophets who spoke God's Word to the people of Israel.

Isaiah (Is)
Jeremiah (Jer)
Lamentations (Lam)
Baruch (Bar)
Ezekiel (Ez)
Daniel (Dn)
Hosea (Hos)
Joel (Jl)
Amos (Am)
Obadiah (Ob)
Jonah (Jon)
Micah (Mi)
Nahum (Na)
Habakkuk (Hb)
Zephaniah (Zep)
Haggai (Hg)
Zechariah (Zec)
Malachi (Mal)

New Testament

The Gospels

These books contain the message and key events in the life of Jesus Christ. Because of this, the Gospels hold a central place in the New Testament.

Matthew (Mt)

Mark (Mk)

Luke (Lk)

John (Jn)

Letters

These books contain letters written by Saint Paul and other leaders to individual Christians or to early Christian communities.

Romans (Rom)

1 Corinthians (1 Cor)

2 Corinthians (2 Cor)

Galatians (Gal)

Ephesians (Eph)

Philippians (Phil)

Colossians (Col)

1 Thessalonians (1 Thes)

2 Thessalonians (2 Thes)

1 Timothy (1 Tim)

2 Timothy (2 Tim)

Titus (Ti)

Philemon (Phlm)

Hebrews (Heb)

James (Jas)

1 Peter (1 Pt)

2 Peter (2 Pt)

1 John (1 Jn)

2 John (2 Jn)

3 John (3 Jn)

Jude (Jude)

Wisdom Books

Acts of the Apostles (Acts)

Revelation (Rv)

Everlasting Life

How can we achieve everlasting, or eternal, life? It is an essential question. In the Gospel of Matthew, Jesus is asked this question by The Rich Young Ruler (Matthew 9:16–26). "Teacher, what good thing shall I do that I may obtain eternal life? And He said to him, 'Why are you asking me about what is good? There is only One who is good; but if you wish to enter life, keep the commandments.'" In this Scripture story, Jesus further explains that attachment to earthly things also separate us from God. Our journey to everlasting life begins with our Baptism.

Christ brings us salvation. Through his suffering, Death, and Resurrection, Jesus Christ saved us from sin and restored us to God's life and love. Just as we believe in Jesus' Resurrection, we have hope in our own resurrection and everlasting life with Jesus Christ after we die. Everlasting life is living in happiness with God forever. As part of the Body of Christ, we follow Christ's teachings and try to live as he did. People who have responded to God's grace and have remained in his friendship will have everlasting life when they die. Those who have lived lives of holiness on earth will immediately share in the joy of heaven and everlasting life. Others whose hearts need to be made perfectly pure will prepare for heaven in Purgatory. These people will grow in holiness necessary to enjoy the happiness of heaven, too.

Salvation History

Salvation is true history. It is not a fairy tale. It is the history of God's plan to save the world from sin and death after the fall of Adam and Eve. The historical books of the Bible tell a story that unfolds over thousands of years. We know that the fall of Adam and Eve separated us from God, but a series of covenants, or contracts, reestablished our relationship with God and prepared us for the coming of his Son, Jesus Christ. It is through Christ that God brings salvation for all who believe in him.

The Covenants

Noah: After the Fall of Adam and Eve, humanity became more separated from God. Noah, however, was an exception. God told him to build an ark to preserve his family and some animals from a flood that was punishment for the world. After the flood, God promised never to destroy the earth again by flood. The rainbow was a sign of God's promise to the world.

Abraham: God called Abraham to leave his own country, promising him a land and to make him a father of many nations. With faith in God, Abraham settled in the Promised Land and became the father of the Jewish people. God's promise to Abraham was perfectly fulfilled in Christ. Through him, God has established a redeemed nation, the Church, given us an everlasting homeland, heaven, and blessed all peoples.

David: The Israelites had reached the Promised Land but broke the commandments. They became jealous of the nations around them. Saul, their first king, was unfaithful. Then, God chose David as king of the Chosen People. God promised David that one of his descendants would reign forever. God's promise to David was perfectly fulfilled in Jesus, Son of David and King of the new Kingdom of God.

The Prophets: Solomon, the son of David, built the Temple but also broke God's commandments. His successors split his kingdom between north and south. In the 6th century BC, the Babylonians captured Jerusalem and the southern kingdom. Throughout this period, God sent prophets such as Elijah, Isaiah, Jeremiah, and Ezekiel. These prophets called the people to repentance, social justice, and peace. They also prophesied a future salvation; a new and everlasting covenant; a Messiah or Christ, 'the anointed one.' God's promise of salvation, made through his prophets, was perfectly fulfilled in Jesus.

John the Baptist: Although the people returned from Babylon, there was no new king. They remained at the mercy of the Persians, the Greeks, and eventually the Romans. Finally, a prophet appeared, John the Baptist, calling the people to repentance and to prepare for the imminent coming of the Messiah

Salvation history is important because it recalls the past and shows God's plan in the present. The story of salvation is not over. This plan of God surrounds us, and we are actively a part of it.

"As it is written in Isaiah the prophet:
Behold, I am sending my messenger ahead of you;
he will prepare your way.
A voice of one crying out in the desert:
'Prepare the way of the Lord,
make straight his paths'" (Mark 1:2–3).

Let the Moral Law Be Your Guide

We make decisions almost every waking moment. But have you ever stopped to think about how many moral decisions your family faces in a typical day? You probably make more moral choices than you know. Some of these choices can be instinctive, or "second nature." Other times, you may need to carefully consider your decision. Jesus gave his disciples the New Commandment as a simple but powerful way to live a moral life. God has given us the guidance we need to choose what is good and right. God's guidance comes in different forms. Together, they make up what we know as the moral law. Review these four expressions of the moral law with your child. Ask your child to tell you what he or she has learned about the revealed law this year.

Four Expressions of the Moral Law

1 The source of all moral law is the divine law, or eternal law. This law is called "eternal" because it is always true and never changes. It is reflected in everything God has created from the beginning of time. The eternal law is "the source, in God, of all law" (CCC 1952).

2 Human beings have an awareness of good and evil, right and wrong, with which we are born. It is God-given, part of our human nature. This is the natural law. The natural law is the law of God within us, which is known by human reason. The natural law is understood through our consciences. The natural law helps us to be in right relationships with God, others, the world, and ourselves. It also helps us understand and follow other expressions of the moral law.

3 God also revealed his law to us in Scripture. This is called revealed law. God's law was first revealed in the Old Testament in the Ten Commandments

he gave to Moses on Mount Sinai. The Ten Commandments express what God has already placed in the human heart in the natural law. God's law is more fully revealed in the New Testament, in the law of love that Jesus taught. This is called the New Law. It is contained in the New Commandment of Jesus (see below).

4 Finally, God gives us civil law and the laws of the Church to guide us. Civil law establishes rules for how we are to live as members of a community. The natural law provides the foundation for the creation of moral and just civil laws. The Church is also a source of moral guidance for us. Through her Tradition, or teaching, the Church helps us understand revealed law and how to live it. The Church also has her own laws to guide us. This is called ecclesiastical law. It includes the precepts of the Church. Review the precepts of the Church with your child, found on page 253 of this book.

New Commandment

Jesus gave us the following commandment. Let it guide all your relationships—at home, at school, in the parish, and in the community.

> *"I give you a new commandment: love one another. As I have loved you, so you also should love one another. This is how all will know that you are my disciples, if you have love for one another."*
>
> *John 13:34-35*

Called to Be Saints

Yes, it is true, everyone in your family can become a saint! Having been made holy by your Baptism and united to Christ, you are actually called to be a saint. Saints were ordinary human beings, just like you, who were faithful disciples of Jesus. They are followers of Christ who lived lives of holiness on earth and now share in eternal life with God in heaven. From the example of the saints' lives, we can learn ways to love God, ourselves, and others. We can learn how to be disciples of Jesus, as the saints were.

Vocations

In Baptism, God calls all of us to serve him. A vocation is God's call to serve him in a particular way. Each baptized person has a vocation to love and serve God. There are specific ways to follow our vocation: the married or single life, the religious life, or the life of an ordained priest or permanent deacon.

Many Catholics live out their vocation as laypeople in the married life or the single life. Through marriage a husband and wife share God's love in a special way with each other and form a new Christian family. They spend much of their time and energy in loving, caring, and sharing their faith with their families, but can also serve others in their parishes, neighborhoods, and communities. Single people often devote themselves to sharing their gifts and talents with others through their work.

Some men and women follow Jesus Christ in the religious life. They are priests, brothers, or sisters who belong to religious communities and make vows or promises to God. They promise: poverty–to live simply as Jesus did, owning no property or personal goods; *chastity*–to live a life of celibacy, remaining single and devoting themselves to the work of God and the Church; *obedience*—to listen carefully to God's direction in their lives by obeying the leaders of the Church and their religious communities.

God calls some baptized men to be priests and permanent deacons. Priests promise to live a life of celibacy, remaining single. This allows them to serve all of God's people.

The Church encourages all members to promote vocations. Here are ten ways we can do it as a family.

Ways to Promote Vocations

- Encourage your children to be involved in the liturgical life of the parish as servers, lectors, musicians, and so on.

- Cultivate an attitude of service by responding as a family to the needs of others. Seek out those in need and find ways to care for them.

- Find opportunities to affirm the gifts and talents of your children and help them relate their gifts to various careers and life choices (including priesthood and religious life).

- On the date of your child's Baptism, talk about the life of the saint for whom the child is named (or the saint's day it is). The saints are people who tried to make a positive difference in the world.

- Visit churches and shrines while on vacation and offer prayers together as a family.

- Discuss your own vocation to family life, explaining that God calls some people to priesthood or religious life, some to marriage, and some to life as single laypeople.

- Share the story of your own vocational choice with your children. Celebrate the occasion of your wedding anniversary as you share the story of your vocation to married life.

Based on *"ABCs of Fostering Vocations,"* United States Conference of Catholic Bishops

Prayer for Vocation

Dear God, you have a great and loving plan for our world and for me. I wish to share in that plan fully, faithfully, and joyfully. Help me to understand what it is you wish me to do with my life. Help me to be attentive to the signs that you give me about preparing for the future. Help me to learn to be a sign of the kingdom, or reign, of God whether I am called to the priesthood or religious life, the single or married life. And once I have heard and understood your call, give me the strength and the grace to follow it with generosity and love.

Amen.

Glossary

Amen (page 182) a word that means "I believe what I just prayed"

apostolic succession (page 56) the authority Christ passed on to the Apostles and their successors, the bishops, from generation to generation, to sanctify, teach, and govern in the Church

Ascension (page 48) the event of Jesus' returning to the Father in heaven

attitude (page 154) a way of thinking that we show in our behavior

bishops (page 96) the successors of the Apostles who carry out the mission, as given to the Apostles by Christ, or teaching, governing, and sanctifying the Church

Cardinal Virtues (page 115) prudence, justice, fortitude, and temperance

common good (page 116) a state of being in which the good of all people is valued by society more than the good of a few

common priesthood of the faithful (page 79) our share in Christ's priesthood through the Sacraments of Baptism and Confirmation; we share in offering prayer and sacrifice to God

Confirmation (page 81) the sacrament in which we receive the Gift of the Holy Spirit in a special way

conscience (page 113) the ability to use reason to know the difference between good and evil, right and wrong

conversion (page 87) turning to God with all one's heart

covenant (page 20) a solemn agreement of faithfulness between God and God's people

deacons (page 96) baptized men ordained by a bishop to serve the Church in worship, governance, and charity

deposit of faith (page 24) the heritage of faith contained in Sacred Scripture and Sacred Tradition, passed on in the Church from the time of the Apostles

devotions (page 74) forms of personal prayer

Divine Revelation (page 28) the way God reveals himself to us

domestic church (page 98) the church in the home, which every Christian family is called to be

free will (page 104) the freedom to choose to do right or wrong

hell (page 40) the state of eternal separation from God

Immaculate Conception (page 44) the teaching that from the very first moment of her life, Mary was free from Original Sin

Incarnation (page 46) the event of the divine Son of God taking on human nature

justice (page 116) respecting the rights of others and supporting their having what is rightfully theirs

justification (page 140) the action of God by which we are freed from sin and reconciled to God

Kingdom of God (page 172) God's reign of justice, peace, and mercy

Last Judgment (page 40) the coming of Jesus Christ at the end of time to judge all people

liturgical year (page 71) the calendar of the liturgies and prayers of the Church

marks of the Church (page 52) one, holy, catholic (universal), and apostolic, as professed in the Nicene Creed

marriage covenant (page 97) the lifelong commitment, entered in the Sacrament of Matrimony between a baptized man and baptized woman, to live as faithful and loving partners

Messiah (page 31) anointed one; Jesus was anointed to bring salvation to the People of God

missionary mandate (page 55) the Church's mission to unite the whole world to Christ

mortal sin (page 130) grave sin that completely turns us away from God

natural law (page 107) a moral sense within us that moves us to seek God and choose what is good and true

New Covenant (page 23) the covenant God made with us through Jesus' Body and Blood at the Last Supper

Original Sin (page 128) the first sin committed by Adam and Eve that weakened human nature and brought ignorance, suffering, and death into the world; we all suffer its effects

Paschal Mystery (page 62) Christ's Passion, Death, Resurrection, and Ascension, through which he accomplished the work of our salvation

People of God (page 31) the people God has been gathering to himself to share in God's life

prayer (page 146) lifting our minds and hearts to God

prayer of intercession (page 162) a prayer in which we ask for something on behalf of another person or group of people

prayer of petition (page 162) a prayer in which we ask something of God

priests (page 96) baptized men ordained by their bishops to serve the Church by preaching and celebrating the Eucharist and other sacraments

prophet (page 80) someone who speaks on behalf of God, reminds people to be faithful to God, defends the truth, and works for justice

psalm (page 166) a poetic prayer designed to be sung or chanted to some kind of musical accompaniment

Purgatory (page 40) a period of time after a person dies when he or she is purified before entering eternity with God

sacramentals (page 66) sacred, or holy, signs and actions that have been instituted by the Church; they prepare us to receive God's grace, especially in the sacraments

Sacraments of Christian Initiation (page 78) Baptism, Confirmation, and Eucharist; these sacraments initiate new members into the Body of Christ, the Church

Sacraments of Healing (page 86) Penance and Reconciliation and Anointing of the Sick; these sacraments give peace and comfort to those suffering from illness or old age

salvation (page 20) the forgiveness of sins and the restoration of friendship with God

sanctifying grace (page 139) God's life in us, which we receive at Baptism

solidarity (page 116) the Christian virtue that involves a love for all people and respects the needs of others and the common good

soul (page 104) the spiritual dimension of our being that gives us life and that lives forever

Ten Commandments (page 120) laws of God's Covenant that provide a model for loving others and living in God's truth

Theological Virtues (page 114) faith, hope, and love

vocation (page 94) the call from God to grow in holiness, share the message of Jesus' life and saving work, and serve one another and the Church

Q&A

Q: What is a covenant?

A: A covenant is a solemn agreement of faithfulness between God and his people. We find stories of God's covenant with Noah, Abraham, and Moses in the Old Testament. *CCC, 70*

Q: What is the New Covenant?

A: The New Covenant is the covenant God made with us through Jesus' sacrifice of his Body and Blood on the Cross for the forgiveness of sins. *CCC, 71, 72*

Q: What is the deposit of faith?

A: The deposit of faith is the heritage of faith contained in Sacred Scripture and Sacred Tradition, passed on in the Church from the time of the Apostles. *CCC, 97, 98*

Q: What is Divine Revelation?

A: Divine Revelation is the way God reveals himself to us. Through the prophets, God prepared his people for the fullness of Divine Revelation—Jesus Christ. *CCC, 315, 319*

Q: Who is the Messiah?

A: The Messiah is Jesus, who was anointed to bring salvation to the People of God. Jesus, whose name means "God saves," is the Messiah because he accomplished this divine mission. *CCC, 452, 453, 455*

Q: What is hell?

A: Hell is the state of eternal separation from God. When we die, we will enter heaven, hell, or Purgatory. *CCC, 1057*

Q: What is Purgatory?

A: Purgatory is a period of time after a person dies when he or she is purified, or becomes more holy, before entering eternity with God. *CCC, 1054*

Q: What is the Last Judgment?

A: The Last Judgment is the coming of Jesus Christ at the end of time to judge all people. *CCC, 1059*

CCC = Catechism of the Catholic Church

Q: What is the Ascension?

A: The Ascension is the event of Jesus' returning to the Father in heaven. *CCC, 659-663*

Q: What is the Immaculate Conception?

A: The Immaculate Conception is the teaching that from the very first moment of her life, Mary was free from Original Sin. She was full of God's Grace. *CCC, 973, 974*

Q: What is the Incarnation?

A: The Incarnation is the event of the divine Son of God taking on human nature in Jesus Christ. The Incarnation is at the center of God's plan of creation and salvation for humanity. *CCC, 460, 479*

Q: Who are the People of God?

A: The People of God are the people God has been gathering to himself to share in God's life. *CCC, 781, 1267*

Q: What is the missionary mandate?

A: The missionary mandate is the Church's mission to unite the whole world to Christ. Our task in proclaiming salvation is to enter into respectful dialogue with those who do not yet accept the Gospel. *CCC, 868*

Q: What is apostolic succession?

A: Apostolic succession is the authority Jesus Christ passed on to the Apostles and their successors, the bishops, from generation to generation, to sanctify, teach and govern in the Church. *CCC, 77, 883, 1087, 1209*

Q: What is the Body of Christ?

A: The Body of Christ is the Church in which God continues to offer his salvation to the entire world. *CCC, 1187, 1195*

Q: What are sacramentals?

A: Sacramentals are sacred, or holy, signs and actions that prepare us to receive God's grace, especially in the sacraments. Sacramentals can be objects, such as blessed rosary beads, or statues, or actions, such as kneeling in the home or making the Sign of the Cross. They can also be certain prayers, such as the Rosary. *CCC, 1677, 1678*

Q: What is the liturgical year?

A: The liturgical year is the calendar of the liturgies and prayers of the Church. The Church year is based on the life of Christ and the celebration of his life in the liturgy. It begins with Advent. The Paschal Triduum is the center of the liturgical year. *CCC, 1194, 1195*

Q: **What are devotions?**

A: Devotions are forms of personal prayer. We encounter God through devotions. They can help us bring us closer to Jesus. *CCC, 1679*

Q: **What are the Sacraments of Christian Initiation?**

A: The Sacraments of Christian Initiation are Baptism, Confirmation, and Eucharist. These sacraments make us members of the Church. *CCC, 1275*

Q: **What is the common priesthood of the faithful?**

A: The common priesthood of the faithful is our share in Christ's priesthood through the Sacraments of Baptism and Confirmation; everything we do becomes a spiritual offering to God when we unite it to the sacrifice of Christ. *CCC, 620, 1533, 1535*

Q: **What are the Sacraments of Healing?**

A: The Sacraments of Healing are Penance and Reconciliation and the Anointing of the Sick. These sacraments reconcile us with God and give us strength and peace. *CCC, 1486*

Q: **What is conversion?**

A: Conversion is a turning to God with all one's heart. It is the work of God's grace within us and leads us to live in a way that is pleasing to God. *CCC, 1490*

Q: **What is a vocation?**

A: A vocation is God's call to each person to serve him in a special way. Our common vocation is to grow in holiness and share the message of Jesus' life and saving work, and to serve one another and the Church. We do this as laypeople consecrated, religious, or ordained ministers. *CCC, 1591, 1592*

Q: **What are the Sacraments at the Service of Communion?**

A: The Sacraments at the Service of Communion are the Sacraments of Holy Orders and Matrimony. Those who celebrate them help the Church grow in holiness through the ministerial priesthood and through married life. *CCC, 1534*

Q: **What is free will?**

A: Free will is the freedom to decide when and how to act. Free will is the gift that, informed by our faith, allows us to freely respond to God's grace and choose the path of beatitude—life with God forever. *CCC, 1711*

Q: What is natural law?

A: Natural law has been planted by God in the heart of every person. It is a rational awareness, a voice of reason, and a moral sense within us to seek God and choose what is good and true. *CCC, 1955, 1956*

Q: What is conscience?

A: A well-formed conscience leads us to use our reason to know the difference between good and evil, right and wrong. When we listen to our conscience, we can hear God speaking, and we must always obey. *CCC, 1713, 1776, 1796*

Q: What are the Theological Virtues?

A: The Theological Virtues are faith, hope, and love have their origin in God. They are gifts from God that help us to live in relationship with the Blessed Trinity and bring us closer to God and increase our desire to be with God forever. *CCC, 1803, 1804, 1830*

Q: What are the Cardinal Virtues?

A: The Cardinal, or Moral, Virtues should guide our actions, emotions, and choices in accordance with reason and faith. The Cardinal Virtues are the virtues of prudence, justice, fortitude, and temperance. *CCC, 1804, 1805*

Q: What is the common good?

A: The common good concerns the life of all people, either as groups or individuals, living in dignity and being afforded social and economic opportunities. It is in our families that we first begin to understand that our own good is directly related to the common good. *CCC, 1947, 1948*

Q: What is justice?

A: Justice enables us to give God and neighbor their due. Justice inspires us to stand up for human rights around the world. *CCC, 1923, 1924*

Q: What are the Ten Commandments?

A: The Ten Commandments are laws of God's Covenant that provide a model for loving others and living in God's truth. *CCC, 1982, 1983*

Q: What is Original Sin?

A: Original Sin is the first sin that weakened human nature and brought ignorance, suffering, and death into the world; we all suffer its effects. *CCC, 1714*

Q: What is mortal sin?

A: Mortal sin is a grave sin that destroys charity, the virtue by which we love God above all things and our neighbor as ourselves, in our hearts. We deliberately and freely choose to do something gravely contrary to God's law, and we know it. *CCC, 1874*

Q: **What is sanctifying grace?**

A: Sanctifying grace is God's life in us that we receive at Baptism. It heals us and makes us holy. *CCC, 2023*

Q: **What is justification?**

A: Justification is the work of God in us, transforming us from sinfulness to holiness. It is granted to us through our Baptism. *CCC, 2020*

Q: **What is prayer?**

A: Prayer is lifting our minds and hearts to God. Prayer is our response to God's call to enter into a relationship with him. *CCC, 2590*

Q: **What is a prophet?**

A: A prophet is someone who speaks on behalf of God reminds people to be faithful to God, defends the truth, and works for justice. *CCC, 64, 65, 75, 201*

Q: **What is a prayer of petition?**

A: A prayer of petition is a prayer in which we ask something of God. This is probably the most common form of prayer. *CCC, 2644*

Q: **What is a prayer of intercession?**

A: A prayer of intercession is a prayer in which we ask for something on behalf of another person or group of people. *CCC, 2644*

Q: **What is a psalm?**

A: A psalm is a poetic prayer designed to be sung or chanted. King David is thought to have written many of the psalms. *CCC, 2585–2589*

Q: **What is a source?**

A: A source is something from which our prayers can be obtained or found; the three sources of prayer are God's Word, the Church's liturgy, and the virtues of faith, hope, and charity. *CCC, 2694*

Q: **What is the Kingdom of God?**

A: The Kingdom of God is God's reign of justice, peace, and mercy. It helps us focus on the here and now—building God's Kingdom today and directs us toward the hope of the Kingdom to come at the end of time. *CCC, 2857*

Q: **What are the liturgical seasons?**

A: Seasons in the calendar year that celebrate special people and events in our Church. The liturgical seasons are Advent, Christmas, Ordinary Time, Lent, the Triduum, and Easter. *CCC, 1158-1173*

Q: Why do we celebrate Advent?

A: Advent is that time of year when we pray with the visions of the prophets because God's plan of salvation was fulfilled in Jesus Christ and renew our hope in the future when we look forward to Christ's Second Coming in glory. *CCC*, 524

Q: Why do we celebrate Christmas?

A: Christmas celebrates the fulfillment of God's promise to send a Messiah. The fulfillment of this promise continues in every liturgy, especially the Eucharistic celebration. *CCC*, 525, 526, 1171

Q: Why do we celebrate Lent?

A: Lent is a season in which we renew our faith. Just as Jesus went out into the desert and fasted for forty days to prepare for his mission, so we renew our call to faith each year, during the forty days of Lent. *CCC*, 1438

Q: What is the Triduum?

A: The Triduum celebrates Jesus' work of redemption in which Passover helps us to understand why we call Jesus the Lamb of God. It is three special days in which we recall the Last Supper, the Death of Jesus on the cross, and God raising Jesus from the dead. *CCC*, 1168

Q: Why do we celebrate Easter?

A: Easter celebrates Jesus' Resurrection and our hope for eternal life in communion with the Blessed Trinity. *CCC*, 1169

Q: What is the mission of Pentecost?

A: Pentecost calls us to be Christ's witnesses in the world, in everything we do. The Holy Spirit has made us his messengers so that we proclaim the truth of the Good News. *CCC*, 696, 715, 731

Q: What is Ordinary Time?

A: Ordinary Time is the longest season in the liturgical year. It is a rich celebration of the events of Jesus' life, his public ministry, and the core of his teachings. *CCC*, 495, 508

Index